The Last Pope
Do Biblical and Catholic Prophecies Point to Pope Francis I?

Many believe that Pope Benedict XVI was number 111 of the 112 popes prophesied by the Catholic saint and Bishop Malachy.

Some have said that there would only be 112, and since Pope Francis I is after Pope Benedict XVI, this could make him 112 — Peter the Roman — the last pope — the pope who Bishop Malachy said would oversee the destruction of Rome?

Could this really be Pope Francis I?

by Bob Thiel, Ph.D.

www.nazarenebooks.com

Is Pope Francis I possibly the Antichrist?

What will happen in the future if he or a successor is?

Edition 1.0 March 2013

The Last Pope
Do Biblical and Catholic Prophecies Point to Pope Francis I?

Could Pope Francis I really be Peter the Roman?

by Bob Thiel, Ph.D.

(also known as COGwriter)

NAZARENE BOOKS is wholly owned by Doctors' Research, Inc. Edition 1.1 20120916

ISBN 978-0-9840871-6-7

NAZARENE BOOKS

For those seeking knowledge
www.nazarenebooks.com

Edition 1.0 March 2013

CONTENTS

Acknowledgements

The author wishes to thank those who helped him to review this book and other books he has written.

Scriptural quotes are mainly taken from the *New King James Version*, sometimes abbreviated as NKJV, throughout this entire text, unless otherwise noted. Copyright © 1979, 1980, 1982 by Thomas Nelson, Inc. Used by permission. All rights reserved.

The *Douay Rheims Bible*, abbreviated as DRB is sometimes also used, as it is an old Roman Catholic accepted standard of the Latin vulgate into the English language. The primary electronic version used here is by permission of William von Peters. The New Jerusalem Bible (NJB) is also sometimes used. Certain photos are under license. Other photos are by Joyce Thiel or public domain sources, such as found via *Wikipedia*.

Introduction and About the Author

The author has studied philosophy, religion, research, science, and prophecy, both formally and informally for several decades. He has a Master's degree from the University of Southern California and a Ph.D. from the Union Institute and University. In the past fifteen years, the author has had scores of articles published on these topics in a variety of print publications such as magazines, newspapers, and journals. He is also a dedicated Christian and Pastor/Overseer of the *Continuing* Church of God (official website is www.ccog.org).

He has been a lifelong researcher and has received several research awards. His recent books, *2012 and the Rise of the Secret Sect*, *Fatima Shock!*, and *Barack Obama, Prophecy, and the Destruction of the United States* have shared unique and helpful prophetic insights to those actually interested in the truth. World events have already aligned with dozens of predictions in those books, including some related to Vatican matters, with one partially fulfilled as recently as March 2013.

He has been married to his wife Joyce since 1981. Together they have made multiple trips to ancient sites in Central America, Asia Minor, Rome, Greece, and elsewhere. This would include visiting such places as Tikal and Iximche in Guatemala; Ephesus, Smyrna, Pergamos, Thyatira, Sardis, Philadelphia, Laodicea, and Patmos in Asia Minor; Vatican City (many times), and Pompeii in the Italian peninsula; Athens, Corinth, Crete, and Rhodes in Greece; Fatima in Portugal; and Constantinople (now Istanbul) and Cappadocia in Turkey. They have also visited ancient ruins in Asia, explored parts of Africa, and visited Washington D.C.

The Thiels have three sons and live near the central California coast.

Because of his passionate interest in both history and prophecy, the author endeavors to make his discoveries available to the public. His writings strive to explain upcoming world events and the peace that is ultimately coming, despite the fact that extremely difficult times are soon ahead. Hundreds of thousands know Dr. Thiel as "COGwriter" and he normally writes one or more articles or online commentaries daily at the popular www.cogwriter.com website. He also functions as the national *Church History and Prophecy Examiner*, for the Examiner.com. In addition, he has a YouTube channel titled BibleNewsProphecy.

Although this book references a variety of terms, including *saint, blessed, venerable, father, mother, brother, sister, prophet, seer,* etc. to identify writers/sources of predictions, this does not mean that the author agrees that those persons truly held those positions. Those terms mainly are quoted from other sources and/or are included, because they may help in identifying these sources historically.

The expression "the last pope" refers to the last individual with major significant religious influence on the earth who comes out of a Greco-Roman church tradition; it does not mean he has to be the last leader to call himself, or even be considered to be, "pope." For example, Benedict XVI could possibly outlive the last pope, and hence some may consider that he was the last pope, or someone else could be proclaimed pope by some cardinals once they realize some of the true objectives of "the last pope."

Also, the term *Roman Catholic* is sometimes used as a distinction from the Eastern Orthodox, the Anglicans, and some others who sometimes use the term *Catholic* to refer to themselves. *Roman* is normally left out when the ties to Rome are obvious by the context, or when something other than the Roman Catholic Church is mentioned.

It should also be understood that the author often comes to different conclusions or interpretations than did some of the reporters/originators of the ancient writings referenced in this book. Yet, before any accuse this book of "Catholic-bashing," realize that **most of the quotes in this book come from Catholic-sources** or sources that the Vatican would approve as appropriate (including the Bible).

Readers are encouraged to look up the sources and compare them to the end-time conclusions in this book.

We're living in exciting and turbulent times. Major national difficulties are eminent in the next few years.

Some have already started to occur. How will the world cope during this time?

Throughout history, civilizations have risen to a ruling superpower and then have fallen a short time later because of economic, social, and/or military difficulties.

Some people have predicted major future global events. Many predictions will come to pass, but many will not.

It would be helpful to know which of these predictions are accurate and when the accurate ones should come to pass. You will be affected and you can make decisions based upon these predictions that may actually save your life.

What if you do not believe in predictions of any type? Does not knowing result in safety? Is ignorance bliss or can preparation provide safety?

Is there any reason that people in the 21st century should bother themselves with ancient writings, drawings, or other sources of prognostication?

In a word — YES.

Whether or not you personally believe that there is any truth in the Bible, Catholic private prophecies, or other predictions, billions of people on this planet do. Because billions of people take these predictions seriously, their beliefs and related actions may ultimately affect you.

How may that happen, you might wonder?

Here is an example. Are you aware that there is a centuries-old prophecy by Muhammad's cousin that claims that just before the return of a great Islamic leader, a "tall black man will assume the reins of government in the West" and command "the strongest army on earth"? Whether or not you feel that this can have anything to do with U.S. President Barack Hussein Obama, if enough Muslims do, those will be more likely to rally behind a religious leader who is destined to take over the nations of the West and force all to become Muslim or die. There are also parallels to this in Catholic prophecies concerning ones sometimes referred to as "the Great Monarch" or "Angelic Pastor."

Historically, certain predictions have come to pass, while others have failed. For example, centuries ago writers calling themselves Catholic predicted airplanes, submarines, television, wars, etc., while others wrongly claimed the world and/or the U.S.A. would be gone by the 19th or 20th century. Would you like to know which prophecies may be correct in the future?

While the author believes that it is the Bible that is divinely inspired (2 Timothy 3:16), he hopes that showing other predictions can give insight into how other sources may view end time events, and that supporters of them may try to make them come to pass. Plus, relating to or citing cultural writings of others is a long used technique in communications (e.g. Acts 17:23, 28; 1 Corinthians 9:20-22).

Even if you do believe in some or all of the predictions of certain writers or some ancient text, but you do not believe in others, the fact is that those who accept predictions that you may not consider to be of value will ultimately have influence on you.

Although the Bible predicts that an age of peace will come, it (along with certain non-biblical sources) actually predicts that a horrible militaristic dictator will first come upon the scene and implement a false ecumenical religion with the assistance of a "miracle-performing" religious leader while enforcing a militaristic "peace" upon the world.

We in the 21st century need to realize that respected news sources are reporting world events that are converging in ways certain to lead to fulfillment of many prophecies. The sources report the news, but almost never understand how these events align with end time prophecies. We face many challenges ahead. Even respected scientists are verifying that bizarre occurrences are expected in a very few years.

Because the entire world will be involved in coming events, wouldn't you like to know now instead of later, what things must and may soon come to pass? Billions of people believe in various predictions. They and various world events point to cataclysmic change in the next decade — change that will significantly affect everyone, even non-believers of prophecies. This book will help you learn what to expect.

Bob Thiel, Ph.D.
Arroyo Grande, California

1. Do Biblical and Catholic Prophecies Warn About Pope Francis I?

Do biblical and certain private Catholic prophecies warn about Pope Francis I?

The Bible warns about a certain religious leader (Revelation 16:13) who will arise in the 21st century (see chapter 10). Biblical prophecies warn that this leader will be at least partially responsible for:

- Causing false worship (Revelation 13:11-16).
- Betraying the end-time Church of Rome, which also results in the destruction of the seven-hilled city (Revelation 17:9, 15-18).
- Getting armies to gather in Armageddon (Revelation 16:13-16) that will fight Jesus (Revelation 19:19-20).
- Persecuting those in the Church of God (Daniel 7:25) as well as others (Revelation 13:15).

Interestingly, Catholic private prophecies also warn of time of an antipope who will encourage false worship, be somehow involved in the destruction of Rome, and support persecution.

While biblical prophecies are not completely specific as to whether or not Pope Francis I is the end time religious leader whom the Bible warns about (as he has not yet performed specified biblically-required signs; cf. 2 Thessalonians 2:9; Revelation 13:13-16), certain Catholic prophecies and writers over the centuries clearly point to Pope Francis I being an antipope.

11

Other writers and theologians, however, have discounted some of those private Catholic prophecies. Some have claimed that the Bishop Malachy prophecy, which is the one that most specifically points to Pope Francis I as "Peter the Roman"[1] and the last pope, is a forgery.[2] Therefore, they claim that no value should be placed in what it, or similar prophecies, say.

Which is correct?

This book details biblical requirements enabling us to determine if Pope Francis I could be the last pope and to see if he is the one to possibly fulfill various private Catholic prophecies.

The Vatican Position on Private Prophecy

This author believes in the authority of the Bible over private prophecies. When there is a conflict, readers are urged to accept the authority of sacred scripture above "private revelation" (which is also the position in the *Catechism of the Catholic Church*[3]). All "private revelations" should be understood within the bounds of scripture. Furthermore, although the Vatican has accepted various private prophecies and apparitions "worthy of belief,"[4] the Vatican "allows freedom in accepting or rejecting particular or private prophecies,"[5] which means that it currently allows people to make up their own minds once they have the facts.

Because the Malachy prophecies of the popes has been fairly accurate, some believe that they were not completely of human origin and that Pope Francis I is the last pope. But, for one example, since his papal list also contains antipopes, it should not be trusted as coming from God (see also chapter 4). Demonic influence on the Malachy list must be considered.

The Bible warns about a false religious leader who will arise in the 21st century, and have ties to Rome, who has many similarties to Peter the Roman of the Malachy prophecies (see chapter 5 for additional details). Because of his timing, it may be that Pope Francis I, despite outward appearances suggesting otherwise, is that false leader and the Malachy private prophecy could be at least partially correct.

The Papal Title Did Not Begin With the Apostle Peter

According to certain Catholic sources, Roman Bishops did not take the title "pope" until the latter portion of the fourth century[6] after the Roman Emperor Gratian basically renounced the title of Pontifex Maximus.[7] The Pontifex Maximus title itself had pagan uses according to Catholic and other scholars.[8]

Since this book is titled *The Last Pope*, the fact that the first to hold the papal title of Pontifex Maximus was not Christian could be of interest to help readers better realize that claiming the title Pontifex Maximus does not make one a genuine Christian. And Catholic scholars agree.[9]

That being said, this book will cite biblical and Catholic writings that warn about one who could be expected to be the last pope.

2. Why Could Pope Francis I be the Last Pope?

On March 13, 2013 Cardinal Jorge Mario Bergoglio, became the Bishop of Rome. He took the name Pope Francis I. He is the first pope from Latin America.

Because of the timing of his papal election, Pope Francis I could possibly fulfill biblical prophecies about a particular False Prophet, the final Antichrist. It should be noted that this author has not felt that way about other popes. In 2009, I clearly wrote that I did not believe that Pope Benedict was the final Antichrist.[10]

If certain Catholic private prophecies are correct, if one connects-the-dots, then Pope Francis I is the last pope and would be the antipope that various Catholics have warned about. While some might find that statement outrageous, it is true if certain private prophecies come to pass at the same basic time.

If Pope Francis I is the final pontiff and antipope, he would have to have certain characteristics (including some that are not immediately apparent) for that role. And his age may argue against him being the one who will do so. We will see.

Who is Pope Francis I?

Pope Francis I was born in Argentina, is a Jesuit, and has Italitan ethnicity:

Born in Buenos Aires in 1936, Bergoglio's father was an Italian immigrant and railway worker from the region around Turin, and he has four brothers and sisters. His original plan was to be a chemist, but in 1958 he instead entered the Society of Jesus and began studies for the priesthood.

Although Jesuits generally are discouraged from receiving ecclesiastical honors and advancement, especially outside mission countries, Bergoglio was named auxiliary bishop of Buenos Aires in 1992 and then succeeded the ailing Cardinal Antonio Quarracino in 1998. John Paul II made Bergoglio a cardinal in 2001, assigning him the Roman church named after the legendary Jesuit St. Robert Bellarmino.[11]

Here is more information about him:

Back in 2005, Bergoglio drew high marks as an accomplished intellectual, having studied theology in Germany. His leading role during the Argentine economic crisis burnished his reputation as a voice of conscience, and made him a potent symbol of the costs globalization can impose on the world's poor. [12]

On November 8, 2005, Bergoglio was elected President of the Argentine Episcopal Conference for a three-year term (2005–2008) by a large majority of the Argentine bishops, which according to reports confirms his local leadership and the international prestige earned by his alleged performance in the conclave. He was reelected on November 11, 2008.[13]

He was considered the "runner-up" in the previous papal election back in 2005.[14]

Historically, there seems to have been a mistrust of electing a Jesuit as pope, and sometimes that order has been considered to be a bit militaristic: "it's common even today for Italian Catholics to refer to the Jesuit General as 'il papa nero,' the black pope."[15]

It should be noted that Jesuits normally do not use that expression themselves, and the term "black" is believed to connotate being hidden. A variety of "conspiracy theorist-types" have implicated the "black pope" as being responsible for many illicit activities.[16] Without trying to address them here, let me state that it is the secretiveness, as well as some known past activities of the Jesuits, that have caused some concerns.[17]

Smoke of Satan: Could Cardinals Elect an Antipope?

Many Catholics believe that an antipope could not be elected as they have confidence that the Roman Cardinals will do what is right.

Some in the media have questioned that and pointed out that many of the current cardinals have character issues and/or have been accused of perhaps improperly covering up sexual and other scandals. Those specifically mentioned in a single report in the *Washington Post* in March of 2013 with such issues included Cardinals Sodano, Bertone, Dolan, Brady, Rigali, Hoyos, Danneels, Mahoney, Law, and Levada.[18]

A group called *Survivors Network of those Abused by Priests* (SNAP) has its own list of cardinals it considers corrupt in some manner or the other:

> SNAP has singled out a "Dirty Dozen" cardinals who are contenders for pope that they consider "to be the worst choices in terms of protecting kids, healing victims, and exposing corruption."

> The members of the "Dirty Dozen" cardinals, according to SNAP, are: Oscar Andres Rodriguez Maradiaga (Honduras), Norberto Rivera (Mexico), Marc Ouellet (Canada), Peter Turkson (Ghana), George Pell (Australia), Tarcisio Bertone (Italy), Angelo Scola (Italy), Leonardo Sandri (Argentina), Dominik Duka (Czech Republic), Sean O'Malley (United States), Timothy Dolan (United States), and Donald Wuerl (United States).[19]

Media reports also mention Cardinals O'Brien and Law as corrupt/tainted, but those two were not eligible to vote in the conclave (nor is it certain which cardinals actually did as the conclave is quite secretive).

While some might consider that the Roman Cardinals are at least believers in Jesus and should be qualified, there have been a couple of statements that suggest that various Catholic leaders are aware of problems within the Vatican as well as among various cardinals.

Notice the following from 1972:

> Pope Paul VI spoke on June 29 at St. Peter's Basilica
> and said: "By means of some fissure, the smoke of Satan has entered the temple of God..."[20]

Thus, it would seem that Pope Paul VI was warning that Satan had influenced various Vatican-related leaders.

Notice also the following, which was reported on March 10, 2010:

> Sex abuse scandals in the Roman Catholic Church are proof that "the Devil is at work inside the Vatican", according to the Holy See's chief exorcist.
>
> Father Gabriele Amorth, 85, who has been the Vatican's chief exorcist for 25 years and says...the consequences of satanic infiltration included power struggles at the Vatican as well as **"cardinals who do not believe in Jesus, and bishops who are linked to the Demon"**.

He added: "When one speaks of 'the smoke of Satan' [a phrase coined by Pope Paul VI in 1972] in the holy rooms, it is all true – including these latest stories of violence and paedophilia."[21]

There are cardinals, and presumably bishops who later became cardinals, that do not believe in Jesus and/or have demonic ties **according to that Vatican-related source.** Therefore, it is not far-fetched to consider that those who elected Pope Francis I could have elected one who is, or will become, demonically-influenced.

Perhaps I should add that in 2010, a publication put out by a Catholic priest, titled *The Fatima Crusader,* strongly suggested that Cardinal Bertone was a liar.[22] So, it is not just secular publications that have cast concerns on the character of those who were involved in the process that selected Pope Francis I.

Choice of the Name Francis

Jorge Mario Bergoglio's choice of the name Francis may have some prophetic ramifications.

How so?

There is a very famous Catholic saint named Francis of Assisi. Francis ended up founding the Franciscan Order. Francis of Assisi is well-loved by many Catholics and some others.

While not ever in total agreement, there has long tended to be a special relationship between that Franciscan Order and Islam.[23]

Working closer with Islam, and ultimately converting those in that faith, has long been a goal of various Catholics. The Bible suggests, that for a time (cf. Revelation 13:4), that Islam may *temporarily* accept some ecumenical Catholicism, before engaging in a battle with the nominally Catholic King of the North (Daniel 11:40).

The Bible (Daniel 11:40-43), Catholic prophecy,[24] and certain Islamic prophecy all suggest that the forces of Islam will lose.[25] Biblical (Daniel 9:27; 11:27) and Islamic prophecy[26] indicates this happens after some type of "peace deal" and during the time of the final Antichrist.

IF getting closer to Islam was in any way involved in the selection of the name Francis I, then this is another reason to watch the current pope.

Why Could Pope Francis I Be the Last Pope?

While there is not yet completely firm proof that Pope Francis I is the last pope, and if he does not perform various signs and wonders, the Bible is clear that he certainly would not be (cf. 2 Thessalonians 2:9; Revelation 13:13-16).

The fact that Pope Francis I studied in Germany, has a connection to Italy, is a Jesuit, has economic interests, and has ecumenical tendencies make him a candidate to consider as the final pope.

But also, by virtue of the timing of his election, Pope Francis I is a candidate to be the final Antichrist (1 John 4:1-3) and False Prophet (Revelation 16:13) of the Bible and the antipope certain Catholic prophecies have warned against (for more details, please see chapter 3).

As far as timing goes, there was a book written in 1966 which contains a published blessing by Pope Paul VI which, consistent with the views of the Bible and early professors of Christ, that God has given humanity 6,000 years to rule itself before Jesus returns to establish His Kingdom. According to biblical chronologies and the records of history since Adam and Eve were put out of the Garden of Eden, this 6,000 years is nearly up. And since the Bible is clear that Jesus does not come until after the False Prophet deceives many (cf. Revelation 13:11-14; 16:13; 19:11-20), he must be in public view before the end of the 6,000 years (information on calculations and other information related to the 6,000 years is in chapter 10).

Related to his timing and Catholic prophecies, if at least one is correct as some understand it, Pope Francis I is the last pope and will oversee the destruction of Rome. There is a list that purportedly was produced by Irish Bishop Malachy in the 12th century naming all future popes which also contains a number of antipopes. Bishop Malachy listed 112, Pope Benedict XVI would have been 111 on that list, which makes Pope Francis I pope 112, the last pope (for more information on that list and controversies related to that list, please go to chapter 4).

As far as ecumenical tendencies, the Bible shows that the False Prophet, who supports the Beast of the Sea (Revelation 13:1-10) and final King of the North (Daniel 11:28-45), will be successful in getting people in the world to worship (Revelation 13:4,8) in a different way (cf. Daniel 11:36-38). Certain Catholic prophecies suggest that this leader will try to suggest that this way is the original catholic faith, which it will not be. It will likely call itself Catholic. Yet, according to biblical and Catholic prophecies, he will betray the city of seven hills (Rome).

Since Pope Francis I has not performed the types of signs and wonders that Revelation 13:13-16 requires (to cite one example) it is not clear that he is the last pope. But, because of the timing of his election and other factors, if he lives long enough, he could be.

3. Do Catholic Prophecies Warn About an Antipope?

Could Pope Francis I be an "antipope"?

Is an "antipope" coming?

Throughout history, various ones who had some association (such as *some* called Paulicians[27] and Waldensians[28]) with the Church of God have believed that the final Antichrist would most likely be the final pope. Of course, if someone calls himself pope for a short-while when the False Prophet is gone, it is possible there could be others after the one this book would tend to label "the last pope."

Technically, the final Antichrist could also be construed as an "antipope" in that he will accept changes to the current Roman Catholic religion that the "King of the North" (Daniel 11:37-40) prefers and promote emperor worship (Revelation 13:14). More on the King of the North can be found in chapter 8 and more on the final Antichrist can be found in chapter 6.

Although some Roman Catholic scholars seem to ignore or discount the idea of a future King of the North in Daniel 11,[29] quite a few Catholic writers expect that an ecumenical pope and a conquering emperor will come on the scene. Throughout history, Catholic writers and prophets have had predictions about future popes and a conquering emperor. More on this emperor can be found in chapter 6.

What is an Antipope?

What is an antipope/anti-pope? Here is a short definition
from *The Catholic Encyclopedia*:

> **Antipope** A false claimant of the Holy See in opposition to a pontiff canonically elected.[30]

While historically most have considered that antipopes falsely claimed the Roman Bishopric when others had it, I would contend that it is reasonable to conclude that one who was elected under false pretenses would also be a false claimant and hence antipope. Or if a pope changed and became demonically-possessed, such as the situation involving the False Prophet of Revelation 16:13, would that not make him an antipope? Most Catholics, at least now, would tend to agree that such a one would be a false claimant to the papal role. If so, that would seem to make him an antipope.

Vatican City (Joyce Thiel)

Although there have not been any recognized antipopes for several centuries, *The Catholic Encyclopedia* shows a list of thirty individuals that have been considered antipopes.[31] This is roughly one for every ten claimed "Bishops of Rome." Thus, the appearance of an antipope should not be considered as impossible.

Catholic Prophets/Writers Have Warned that a Major "Antipope" is to Come

Various Catholic prophecies warn that a major "antipope" and major schism is to come. Since there has not been an antipope since the 15th century, for numerous reasons these could be interpreted to mean that a 21st century pope will be an antipope who will implement changes:

> *Anne Catherine Emmerick* (May 13, 1820): I saw again a new and odd-looking Church which they were trying to build. There was nothing holy about it...THIS IS BABEL.[32]

> *Yves Dupont* {writer interpreting A. Emmerick}: They wanted to make a new Church, a Church of human manufacture, but God had other designs...The Holy Father shall have to leave Rome, and he shall die a cruel death. An anti-pope shall be set up in Rome.[33]

> *Anne Catherine Emmerich* (January 12, 1820): There is now some question of Protestants

sharing in the government of the Catholic clergy.[34]

Anne Catherine Emmerich (July 1820): I came to the church of Peter and Paul (Rome) and saw a dark world of distress, confusion, and corruption...[35]

Anne Catherine Emmerich (January 27, 1822): I saw many Christians returning to the bosom of the Church, entering through the walls. That Pope will be strict, he will remove the lukewarm, tepid Bishops — but it will be a long time before this happens.[36]

Anne Catherine Emmerich (October 22, 1822): I saw in Germany among the worldly-wise ecclesiastics, and enlightened Protestants, plans formed for the blending of all religious creeds...[37]

Anne Catherine Emmerich (April, 1823): They built a large, singular, extravagant church which was to embrace all creeds with equal rights: Evangelicals, Catholics, and all denominations, a true communion of the unholy with one shepherd and one flock. There was to be a Pope, a salaried Pope without possessions.[38]

Melanie Mathieu (19th century): Rome will lose faith and become the seat of Antichrist.[39]

Jeanne le Royer (died 1798): I see that when the Second Coming of Christ approaches a bad priest will do much harm to the Church.[40]

St. Gregory the Great, Pope (d. 604): In those days, near the end...an army of priests and two-thirds of the Christians will join the Schism.[41]

Yves Dupont {reader and collector of Catholic prophecies}: "prophecies are quite explicit about the election of an anti-pope...Many prophecies predict an anti-pope and a schism ".[42]

Catholic priest and writer R. Gerald Culleton (20th century): A schism of short duration is destined to break out...An antipope, of German origin, is to be set up, and finally Rome itself will be destroyed".[43]

Frederick William Faber (died 1863): Antichrist...Many believe in a demonical incarnation--this will not be so--but he will be utterly possessed...His doctrine as apparent contradiction of no religion, yet a new religion...He has an attending pontiff, so separating regal and prophetic office.[44]

Blessed Joachim (died 1202): Towards the end of the world Antichrist will overthrow the Pope and usurp his See.[45]

Merlin (7th century): There will come a German Anti-Pope. Italy and Germany will be sorely troubled. A French King will restore the true Pope.[46]

St. Francis of Assisi (died 1226): There will be an uncanonically elected pope who will cause a great Schism, there will be divers thoughts preached which will cause many, even those in the different orders, to doubt, yea even agree with those heretics which will cause My order to divide, then will there be such universal dissentions and persecutions that if these days were not shortened even the elect would be lost.[47]

Capuchin Friar (18th century): During these calamities the Pope shall die…three popes shall be simultaneously elected…the third…by force of arms, shall be placed on the throne.[48]

Priest E. Sylvester Berry (published 1920): It has been a matter of history that the most disastrous periods for the Church were times when the Papal throne was vacant or when anti-popes contended with the legitimate head of the Church. Thus shall it be in those evil days to come.[49]

Catholic writer and priest P. Huchedé (19th century): …the false prophet…will not be a king, nor a general of an army, but a clever apostate, fallen from episcopal dignity. From being an apostle of the Gospel he will become the first preacher of the false messiah...[50]

Priest Herman Kramer (20th century): This false prophet possibly at the behest of Antichrist usurps the papal supremacy.[51]

Catholic writers Ted and Maureen Flynn (1993): Catholic prophecy warns us of severe problems threatening the papacy in these end times...An Antipope will seize papal authority...It will be those who hold fast to the truths of the faith who will be labelled as the perpetuators of this horrible schism, according to some visionaries.[52]

Priest Paul Kramer reported: In 1999...Malachi Martin stated...that Our Lady's words were very dry and specific and they foretold of *a future "pope" (not the true Pope, but a heretical antipope) who would be completely under the control of the devil.*[53]

Priest Paul Kramer (21st century): **The errors of Orthodoxy and of Protestantism will be embraced by that false church, it will be an ecumenical church because the Anti-Pope will be recognized by the world** — not by the faithful, but by the world — by the secular world and the secular governments. The Anti-Pope will be recognized as the legitimate Pope of the "church," and the legitimate head of the Vatican State. That "church" will be united with all the false religions.[54]

Priest Paul Kramer (21st century): The counterfeit "Catholic" Church — the counter-church, the anti-church — the mystery of the dragon, whose tail swept down a third of the "stars of Heaven," i.e. one third of the Catholic hierarchy under the leadership of a heretical antipope.[55]

Priest Herman Kramer (20th century): In accord with the text this is unmistakably a PAPAL ELECTION . . . But at this time the great powers may take a menacing attitude to hinder the election of the logical and expected candidate by threats of a general apostasy, assassination or imprisonment of this candidate if elected. This would suppose an extremely hostile mind in the governments of Europe towards the Church, because an extended interregnum in the papacy is always disastrous and more so in a time of universal persecution. If Satan would contrive to hinder a papal election, the Church would suffer great travail... one...destined for the papacy at the time will institute the needed reforms. A general council may decree the reforms...The lax clergy at the time will extol the conditions then existing...The dragon is a symbolic term for the evil world powers...They will try to make the Church a "state church" everywhere. This is only possible if they can subject the pope to their wills and compel him to teach and rule as they direct. That would be literally devouring the papacy.[56]

Catholic author and collector of prophecies D. Birch (20th century): Many, many, of the prophecies refer to an Antipope for sometime in the future during which great calamities occur to the Church.[57]

Even the Catholic saint "Pope Gregory the Great" warned that he believed that the time would come when most Catholics would fall for a changed church (which he called a "schism") in the time of the end. Would this not take a leader that would be, or at least be like, an antipope or the final Antichrist?

As the list above shows, there are many Catholic writers/saints who have warned of some type of an antipope, maybe even the False Prophet, who could be ecumenical, would lead a compromised church, and may listen to the powers of governments in Europe and, possibly, elsewhere.

The Bible, itself, warns of a time when a European Beast will make some type of deal with an ecumenical Roman religious leader (the False Prophet) and later turn on a compromised church (cf. Revelation 17:15-18; 19:20).

An Ecumenical Pope is Prophesied

On the other hand, there are a variety of Catholic prophecies that seem to look forward to an ecumenical pope. This pope will endorse a European leader who comes into power after civil unrest in Europe. This European leader is to establish a new order within Catholicism and essentially eliminate Islam:

Bl. Anna-Maria Taigi (19th century): France shall fall into a frightful anarchy. The French shall have a desperate civil war in the course of which even old men will take up arms. The political parties, having exhausted their blood and their rage without being able to arrive at any satisfactory settlement, shall agree at the last extremity to have recourse to the Holy See. Then the Pope shall send to France a special legate. . . In consequence of the information received, His Holiness himself shall nominate a most Christian King for the government of France...[58]

Bl. Anna Maria Taigi (19th century) ...described to me the great ordeal ahead. Rome would be battered by revolutions...Millions of men would die by the sword in war and civil strife, other millions would perish in unforeseen death. Then entire nations would return to the unity of the Church, and many Turks, Pagans and Jews would be converted and their fervour cover with confusion the original Christians. In one word she told me that our Lord was intending to cleanse the world and His Church...[59]

Brother John of the Cleft Rock (1340): The White Eagle (Great Monarch), by order of the Archangel Michael, **will drive the crescent from Europe** where none but Christians will remain...There will no longer be...Schismatics...[60]

St. Bridget of Sweden (died 1373): The Eagle...He will destroy the Jewish and Mahometan sects.[61]

Telesphorus of Cozensa (died 1388): A powerful French monarch and French pope will regain the holy land after terrible wars in Europe, convert the world, and bring universal peace.[62]

D. Birch (20th century): Civil war will break out in France and Italy...The Great King will be crowned Holy Roman Emperor by the reigning Pope. The Great King will establish Peace and justice in civil matters on a worldwide basis, and protect the primacy of the Church in spiritual matters. The former disciplines of the Church are fully restored and order is re-established...[63]

St. Francis de Paul (1470): The time is coming when the Divine Majesty will visit the world with a new religious order of the holy Cross-bearers... This shall be the last religious order in the Church, and will do more good for our holy religion than all other religious institutions. By force of arms he shall take possession of a great kingdom. **He shall** destroy the sect of Mahomet, **extirpate all** tyrants and **heresies**. He will bring the world to a holy mode of life. There will be one fold and one Shepherd. He shall reign until the end of time...[64]

Comments from writer D.A. Birch on the above from his book: Francis...speaks in a series of letters to Simeon de Limena, Count of Montalto in great detail of a future Great Monarch who will be a Roman Emperor. Limena was a great patron of St. Francis' order and also a great military protector of the Church...He is described as founding a new religious order. To the reader this may sound like he also becomes a priest. That is not the case. What happens is that he founds a religious order, part of which contains military men who take religious vows. He will be the head of the military arm of this order. In this sense it will be like the Knights Templar of the Middle Ages.[65]

D. Birch (commenting further in his book): Many of the prophecies speak of the fact that the Great King at first will not be well-liked, especially by the French clergy.[66]

St. Methodius (circa 385): A time will come when the enemies of Christ will boast...Then a Roman emperor will arise in great fury against them . . . Drawing his sword, he will fall on the foes of Christianity and crush them.[67]

Laurence Ricci, S.J. (died 1775): At a time when the whole world seems doomed, God will intervene. With His aide a valiant duke will arise from the ancient German house which was humiliated by the French monarch. This great ruler will restore stolen Church property. Protestantism will cease and the Turkish empire will end. This duke will be the most powerful monarch on earth. At a gathering of men noted for piety and wisdom **he will, with the aid of the Pope, introduce new rules,** and ban the spirit of confusion. Everywhere there will be one fold and one shepherd.[68]

Notice that Francis de Paul prophesied that there will be a new essentially Roman Catholic religious order that will do more good for the Roman Catholic Church than all other religious institutions as it will eliminate nearly all opposition. This is apparently because the King of the North will successfully work with the Pope to make the world nominally Catholic.

However, notice that some of the Catholic clergy will at first oppose this new order and these changes to Catholicism, but that the pope (probably the final one, and possibly the current one) will embrace them.

While some Catholic prophecies praise a new religious order, others indicate that a new type of Catholicism will not be true to some of its beliefs. Some Catholics have felt that some of their "ecumenical leaders" have not been truly faithful to the beliefs of the Church of Rome.

Notice what some other Roman Catholics have written about future ecumenical plans:

Oba Prophecy: It will come when the Church authorities issue directives to support a new cult, when priests are forbidden to celebrate in any other, when the highest positions in the Church are given to perjurers and hypocrites, when only the renegades are admitted to occupy those positions.[69]

D.A. Birch (20th century): *"The Pope calls an Ecumenical Council which will be viewed as the greatest in the history of the Church. The world is spiritually and materially prosperous as never before and many Jews, Mohammedans, heathens and heretics will enter the Church"*.[70]

Venerable Bartholomew Holzhauser (Born in the 17th century, in Germany): God will bind Satan for a number of years until the days of the Son of Perdition...there will be an ecumenical council which will be the greatest of all councils. **By the grace of God, by the power of the Great Monarch, and by the authority of the Holy Pontiff, and by the union of the most devout princes, atheism and every heresy will be banished from the earth.** The Council will define the true sense of Holy Scripture, and this will be believed and accepted by everyone. [71]

Priest Herman Kramer (20th century): ...the Apocalypse...The thunders may mean the dogmatic declarations of the Church against infidels expressed in an ecumenical council...such as that of...the Infallibility of the Pope...The Seven Thunders may then be declarations of **an ecumenical council clearing up all that was left unfinished by the magisterial office of the Church,** before God will permit Satan to exert his supreme efforts to destroy her from without.   The Seven Thunders will strengthen the faithful and loyal clergy...[72]

The Bible teaches that the Seven Thunders happen near the end (cf. Revelation 10:1-4), so this ecumenical council would be expected to be near the end. It also teaches that the successful ecumenical religion (Revelation 13:4,8) will not have God's approval (Revelation 14,18).

Yet, certain private prophecies seem to praise the success of this ecumenical movement:

> *Blessed Anna-Maria Taigi* (19th century): Whole nations will come back to the Church and the face of the earth will be renewed. Russia...and China will come into the Church.[73]

> *St. Bridget* (14th century): Before Antichrist comes, the portals of Faith will be opened to great numbers of pagans.[74]

> *Venerable Magdalene Porzat* (died 1850) (Great Monarch)...shall...restore to their dominions the legitimate kings. A just and pious man born in Galacia shall be the Supreme Pontiff: then the whole world will be united and

prosperous. One faith only and one emperor shall reign over the whole earth.[75]

Cardinal La Roque (c. 18th century): A regeneration of Faith will appear in Asia.[76]

Mother Alphonse Eppinger (1867): After God has purified the world faith and peace will return. Whole nations will adhere to the teachings of the Catholic Church.[77]

Pope Leo XIII (1893): To take care, therefore, of the preservation and propagation of the Catholic religion among the Hindus, a Hindu clergy has to be formed that could administer the sacraments and govern the Christian people properly, no matter how menacing the times...Be sure that the role of Christianity in such remote regions becomes well known. Make your people understand that something must be done for the Hindus.[78]

We see from the above that certain Catholics expect those in China, Russia, India, and elsewhere to accept their religion in the end.

But it should also be pointed out that there are Chinese and Hindu prophecies that suggest that the Chinese and Hindus will accept false militaristic and/or religious leaders.

First notice two Hindu-related sources:

Vijay Kumar (21st century): For the society to climb back to its pristine glory of the golden era... even the meek would handle metal (pick arms). Whatever the poor and the downtrodden lay their hands upon would become their weapon....people await with abated breath the coming of Bhagwan Kalki...one who delivers the mankind from the existing ills of today. Bhagwan Kalki would be a spiritual master of the highest order with the deadly combination of a wise dictator (Chanakya of the modern era)...[79]

Hindu Prophecies: In all, the Hindu text of Kalki Purana is comprised of 6100 verses describing ... Kalki, who is considered the last Avtar or incarnation of Vishnu or the Supreme Being, who will establish the Age of Truth or Age of Purity on Earth...As agreed by all the religious prophecies, the Awaited One will not be a man of peace like Jesus Christ or Buddha, but a man of war who will destroy evil and establish righteousness on the earth.[80]

Furthermore, notice the following Chinese prophecies from the time of the Tang Dynasty (618-907 A.D.):

Beautiful people come from the West. Korea, China and Japan are gradually at peace.[81]

All negative forces are subservient... China now has a saint. Even if he is not that great a hero.[82]

So, apparently the Chinese people have a prophecy that they will accept leaders "from the West," that the Chinese will have a saint (not something the Chinese normally have), and that this saint is not really that great. Does not this sound like the Chinese may have a prediction that they are destined to accept the Beast and the False Prophet to rise up in Europe (which certainly is West of China)?

It would seem likely that some of the leadership in India and China may point to some prophecies from their own cultures as proof that they are to go along with the final compromised "Catholic" leaders.

But this acceptance of the "Catholic" leaders will not last. According to biblical prophecy, those ends of the earth of the far north (Russia) and east (China) will fight the final European, "daughter of Babylon," "King of the North" (e.g Jeremiah 50:41-43; Ezekiel 39:1-2; Daniel 11:44).
Interestingly, there is even a Russian prophecy that suggests that Russia and China will get together to fight Europe.[83]

So, although certain Catholics are looking to a time that an ecumenical pontiff will appear and their faith spread, this will be more dangerous than most realize.

A compromising "ecumenical" bishop or cardinal is expected to be the False Prophet of Revelation.

Could this be Pope Francis I?

4. The Malachy Prophecies

There is one private Catholic prophetic writing that, if taken at face value, points to Pope Francis I being the last pope. And this is the famous list of popes that an Irish Bishop claimed to get from a vision.

Statue of Bishop Malachy (Patricia Drury)

In the 12th century, a bishop named Malachy (who was later canonized as a saint by Rome) predicted, with what some believe is complete accuracy, every pope since 1143. When Malachy's list became public in the 16th century, it was considered to have been so accurate in predicting the 12th – 16th century pontiffs, that some thought it had not been written until the

16th century. A total of 112 popes (including several antipopes) were predicted.

Here is what *The Catholic Encyclopedia* reported about it:

> The most famous and best known prophecies about the popes are those attributed to St. Malachy. In 1139 he went to Rome to give an account of the affairs of his diocese to the pope, Innocent II, who promised him two palliums for the metropolitan Sees of Armagh and Cashel. While at Rome, he received (according to the Abbé Cucherat) the strange vision of the future wherein was unfolded before his mind the long list of illustrious pontiffs who were to rule the Church until the end of time. The same author tells us that St. Malachy gave his manuscript to Innocent II to console him in the midst of his tribulations, and that the document remained unknown in the Roman Archives until its discovery in 1590 (Cucherat, "Proph. de la succession des papes", ch. xv). They were first published by Arnold de Wyon, and ever since there has been much discussion as to whether they are genuine predictions of St. Malachy or forgeries. The silence of 400 years on the part of so many learned authors who had written about the popes, and the silence of St. Bernard especially, who wrote the "Life of St. Malachy", is a strong argument against their authenticity, but it is not conclusive if we adopt Cucherat's theory that

they were hidden in the Archives during those 400 years.

These short prophetical announcements, in number 112, indicate some noticeable trait of **all future popes from Celestine II, who was elected in the year 1143, until the end of the world**. They are enunciated under mystical titles. Those who have undertaken to interpret and explain these symbolical prophecies have succeeded in discovering some trait, allusion, point, or similitude in their application to the individual popes, either as to their country, their name, their coat of arms or insignia, their birth-place, their talent or learning, the title of their cardinalate, the dignities which they held etc.[84]

While its original date is hard to absolutely prove (I tend to accept the 12th century date), many of the post 16th century predictions on Malachy's list have apparently come true. Some Catholics have written the following about it:

...a list...attributed to St. Malachy...has given fitting descriptions of every pope since the 16th century, when it was discovered.[85]

...the vast majority of Malachy's predictions about successive Popes is amazingly accurate.[86]

St. Malachy named all the popes from the year 1130 to the end of time...On St. Malachy's

1966 schedule, we will only have four more popes to follow Paul.[87]

Since Pope Paul VI in 1966, there have been four popes: John Paul I, John Paul II, Benedict XVI, and Pope Francis I.

The Malachy List Was Not From God

Certain Catholics believe that the Malachy list was divinely inspired. This also seems to be the position of the Protestant prophetic writer Hal Lindsey who in February 2013, while discussing the Malachy list, publicly stated:

> I think that Saint Malachy must have been a believer.[88]

Many, myself included, do not believe that the list was from God.

Others make light of the Malachy list for a variety of reasons. Even the expression "malarkey" may have originated as a derivative of the word Malachy,[89] possibly because of how some viewed Malachy's writings. Malarkey signifies worthlessness.

Many researchers and theologians currently do not believe that the Malachy list was actually produced by him. Some claim that it was not even written until shortly before its discovery in the 16th century.[90] Various ones claim that the list is not authentic.[91] Certain, but not all, modern Catholic sources have claimed "the list attributed to St. Malachy" is "probably a forgery."[92]

This is partially based upon the fact that it seems odd to many that if the list was compiled in the 12th century that it would be unknown for so long and/or that it suggests the destruction of the Church of Rome prior to the return of Jesus.[93] The list does not seem to be referred to in other writings from or about Malachy prior to the 16th century, so this has cast many doubts. Some believe that the list itself was put together by supporters of a 16th century pope in order to resolve certain papal controversies at the time. Some have also suggested that the list was too accurate for the popes in office the first few centuries after it was claimed to have been produced, and thus had to be written after they were in office.

But others point out the overall accuracy of the list.

Yet, it needs to be understood that Malachy's list includes several leaders that the Roman Catholics call antipopes (e.g. Clement VII, Benedict XIII, Felix V, Alexander V, etc.[94]). Those are inserted sometimes together as opposed to always being in strict chronological order.

> *Priest Connor*: [W]hen Malachy visited Pope Innocent II in Rome in 1139, he was given a vision of all the Holy Fathers of the future…**A study of the entire prophecy shows that fulfillment is made possible only by including anti-popes**…[95]

The fact that Malachy's list is NOT completely accurate should show us that the list was not inspired by God. The fact that its accuracy is at least partially dependent upon the inclusion of antipopes in the 15th century, however, suggests that the list was not likely to have been originally composed in the 16th century: including antipopes would seem to not have been particularly helpful for the supporters of a pontiff at the time.

However, the Malachy list is accurate enough that it would seem possibly that some supporters of the False Prophet may, for a time, point to it as further proof that the final Church of Rome is the proper church, especially if they do not accept that "Peter the Roman" is being warned against (which, from a biblical perspective he seems to be; for further detail, please see chapter 5). This could be a factor in many people being deceived.

[It seems possible that the False Prophet (like most other Catholic bishops have) may (based more on tradition than fact) could claim that there was an unbroken succession of bishops in Rome from Peter onwards, that there have been bishops of Rome from the 2nd through 21st centuries (which is essentially true, though some were in France), and that since Malachy's list has somewhat accurately predicted every pope since the middle of the 12th century (which is not quite true as the list includes what Roman Catholics would consider to be false or "antipopes" without indicating that most of them would be false), that therefore the final changed

Roman Catholic Church is the one true Christian faith (and none should believe that, though many will).]

It should be understood that since God did not directly inspire the Malachy prophecies, it is possible that parts are intentionally wrong, in the sense that Pope Francis I, while seemingly number 112 on the list, actually is nowhere on the list and another will rise up who will be more like the prediction for the last pope. Satan is a deceiver and will use the Malachy list as part of his deception one way or the other.

Pope Paul VI, Pope John Paul, Pope John-Paul II, and Pope Benedict XVI?

Most of the Malachy list contains two-three word descriptions in Latin, but the last pope "Petrus Romanus" has a much longer description.

Gens peruerſa.	Animal rurale.	Flos florum.
In tribulatione pacis.	Roſa Vmbriæ.	De medietate lunæ.
Lilium & roſa.	Vrſus uelox.	De labore ſolis.
Iucunditas crucis.	Peregrinᵖapoſtolic⁹.	Gloria oliuæ.
Montium cuſtos.	Aquila rapax.	In pſecutione. extre-
Sydus olorum.	Canis & coluber.	ma S.R.E.ſedebit.
De flumine magno.	Vir religioſus.	Petrus Romanus, qui
Bellua inſaciabilis.	De balneis Ethruriæ.	paſcet oues in mul-
Pœnitentia glorioſa.	Crux de cruce.	tis tribulationibus:
Raſtrum in porta.	Lumen in cœlo.	quibus tranſactis ci-
Flores circundati.	Ignis ardens.	uitas ſepticollis di-
De bona religione.	Religio depopulata.	ruetur, & Iudex tre-
Miles in bello.	Fides intrepida.	mēdus iudicabit po
Columna excelſa.	Paſtor angelicus.	pulum ſuum. Finis.

Some of Malachy's Statements in Latin

In 1966, Peter Bander produced a book titled *The Prophecies of St. Malachy* which provides information in English about the list, including those popes/antipopes who he/others felt met the criteria of the Latin statements. The inside cover of it claims:

> **Peter Bander**…Through the good services of Archbishop Cardinale, he has received the cooperation of the Vatican Archives, and the result is the most authoritative and enlightening edition of the prophecies ever to have appeared.[96]

Archbishop H.E. Cardinale was one time "Apostolic Nuncio to Belgium and Luxenbourg" and former "Apostolic Delegate to Great Britain" wrote the Forward in the book. He calls the book a "fascinating study" which includes the identity of popes and "antipopes."[97]

At the time the book was published, Pope Paul VI was pope and he identified him with the 108th statement from Malachy *FLOS FLORUM* and stated:

> Malachy's legend appears to be an obvious allusion to the Pope's amorial bearings which show three fleurs-de-lis.[98]

The above does not immediately strike one as totally obvious as it could apply to many others. Peter Bander then immediately wrote:

> The following four prophecies have yet to be fulfilled.[99]

Recall that the above was published in 1966. The four popes since Paul VI, were John Paul I, John Paul II, Benedict XVI, and possibly Pope Francis I.

Here is what was the 109th prediction in the Malachy list with a translation supplied by Peter Bander:

> DE MEDIETATE LUNAE
> Of the half moon[100]

While Peter Bander's "speculations" (which involved the Muslims[101]) about what this might mean did not come to pass, the reality is the Pope John Paul I became pontiff on August 26, 1978 near a half moon (August 25, 1978) and died a month later on September 28, 1978 slightly after the half moon (September 24, 1978). Some have suggested that this means his pontificate may have somewhat fulfilled this Malachy prediction.

Here is what was the 110th prediction in the Malachy list:

> DE LABORE SOLIS[102]

Here is the translation and a comment from Peter Bander about the above Malachy writing, beginning with two translations:

> (a) From the toil of the sun
> (b) Of the eclipse of the sun
>
> The election of this Pope will probably take place within the next two decades. [103]

Since Pope John-Paul II was born on the day of a large partial solar eclipse (May 18, 1920) and was buried on the day of a solar eclipse (April 8, 2005), he definitely had something in common with the number 110 predicted pontiff.[104]   He became pontiff on October 16, 1978.

The apparent accuracy of the Malachy predictions for John Paul II and certain others are one of the reasons I do not believe that the list was merely a human forgery as pontiff do not choose the timing of their death or burial.

Here is what was the 111th prediction in the Malachy list with a translation by Peter Bander:

> GLORIA OLIVEA
> The glory of the olive[105]

Notice what was written decades prior to Joseph Ratzinger becoming Pope Benedict XVI by Peter Bander:

> The Order of St. Benedict has claimed by tradition that this pope will come from within the Order...The Order of St. Benedict is known as the OLIVETANS...[106]

Although Joseph Ratzinger did not come from the Benedictine order, the choice of the name "Benedict" could be seen to be consistent with the Malachy prediction about pope number 111.

While some may argue that Josephy Ratzinger could have picked the name Benedict on purpose to fulfill the Malachy prophecy, the fact that he has claimed on 2/28/13 that he would give unconditional obedience to the pontiff that would replace him — one who could be an antipope and who is supposed to reign during the period that leads to the destruction of Rome — suggests that perhaps he did not pick the name "Benedict XVI" to intentionally fulfill the Malachy prophecy as it would not seem that he holds great credence in the list. He claimed he picked the name because of Benedict XV. But some still consider that his choice of the name Benedict added glory to the Benedictine order.

Benedict XVI, Number 111?

Catholic Private Prophecy Might Be Consistent with Pope Benedict's Resignation

Malachy's writing said nothing more about pontiff 111 than "the glory of the olive,"but other Catholic writings *may* have.

Pope Benedict XVI resigned his pontificate effective February 28, 2013. If certain private prophecies prove to be somewhat accurate, his resignation could possibly lead to the fulfillment of them.

Certain Catholic prophecies state that prior to the end of the reign of a pope, another pope will flee and ultimately die. Whether or not due to a resignation, proper or improper pontifical election, and/or some other factors, this suggests that two pontiffs would exist at the end (especially if the Malachy list is complete).

If these prophecies are accurate, this may indicate that this could happen with the Pope Emeritus, who is elderly and German. Therefore, the following are Catholic prophecies that might somewhat apply to the one who was Pope Benedict XVI (whose name was Joseph Ratzinger prior to becoming pope):

> *Nun Emmerich* (19th century): I also saw the Holy Father-- God-fearing and prayerful. Nothing left to be desired in his appearance, but he was weakened by old age and by much suffering.[107]

Abbot "Merlin" Joachim (died 1202): ...the glorious Pontiff, whose name will begin with R...[108]

Helen Wallraff (19th century): Some day a pope will flee from Rome in the company of only four cardinals . . . and they will come to Koeln [Cologne].[109]

Nostradamus (16th century): The great star will burn for seven days. The clouds will cause two suns to appear: The big mastiff will howl all night When the great Pontiff shall change his country.[110]

The Prophecy of Premol (5th century): And I see the King of Rome and his Cross and his tiara, shaking the dust off of his shoes, and hastening his flight to other shores. Thy Church, O Lord, is torn apart by her own children. One camp is faithful to the fleeing Pontiff, the other is subject to the new government of Rome which has broken the tiara. But Almighty God will, in His mercy, put an end to this confusion and a new age will begin. Then, said the Spirit, this is the beginning of the End of Time.

Comment: From this prophecy, it is clear that the true Church will be faithful to the Pope in exile; whereas the new Pope in Rome will be, in fact, an anti-pope...a large number of Catholics will be misled into accepting the leadership of the anti-pope.[111] {Note the comment is from the Catholic writer Dupont personally}.

Of course, the name Ratzinger began with an "R." Being called the "glorious Pontiff" could possibly tied with the Malachy prophecy since the 111th pontiff on the list was somehow glorious ("the glory of the olive").

The Prophecy of Premol claims it is related to the end of time, therefore, if accurate, it would be consistent with the end of the Malachy list. Now, if Pope Benedict lives long enough and later flees and goes to Cologne (Germany), he might fulfill those prophecies. The fact that he intends to keep the name Benedict XVI and also be referred to as pope or pontiff emeritus[112] is consistent with the view that, despite his resignation he, in at least one sense, will be one of two popes. And this idea of two popes has caused unease among some as the following suggests:

> He will continue to wear a white cassock, be known as Benedict...the existence of two men who are addressed as "your holiness" changes the ecclesiastical atmospherics. For a lot of traditionalist Catholics, two "popes" (even if one is emeritus) is one pope too many.[113]

Traditionally in Catholicism, the wearing of the white cassock has been reserved for the pope. So, this seems consistent with the view that there could be two "popes," with one perhaps being an antipope.

More About Malachy's List

While Malachy himself seemed to indicate that his list included all the future popes, it should be noted that decades ago, Peter Bander wrote that Malachy's list could allow that there would be other popes, not on the list, prior to the last one. Notice:

> Some medieval interpreters have gone out of their way to stress that Malachy in his prophecies does not specifically mention that no Popes reign between *Gloria Olivae* and the last *Petrus Romanus*; nor on the other hand does he mention that there will be others.[114]

So, the above (which is also consistent with *The Catholic Encyclopedia*[115]) does give the Malachy list supporters "wiggle room" if there remains more than one pope left. But if there is only one, then Pope Francis I would seemingly be the False Prophet of Revelation 16:13.

Notice also:

> *Priest Gaudentius Rossi* (19th century): According to St. Malachy, then, only ten, or at most eleven, popes remain to be in future more or less legitimately elected. We say more or less legitimately elected, because out of those future popes it is to be feared that one or two will be unlawfully elected as anti-popes.[116]

There have not been any recognized "antipopes" since Felix V's time in 1439-1449.[117] Thus, if Priest

Rossi's understanding on those points is correct, it would seem then that Pope Francis I, who is the last pope on Malachy's list would be an anti-pope as there are no others left on the Malachy list.

Because of Benedict XVI's resignation, "The Vatican has been rewriting the rules to cope with an almost unprecedented situation..."[118] This could be interpreted to possibly mean to some that Pope Francis I's election was somehow improper (as could certain "behind-the-scenes" discussions). This could be consistent with certain beliefs, like the statement from Priest Rossi, about the antipope being "more or less legitimately elected."

Peter the Roman

The most famous name on the Malachy list is probably
the last one. Commonly referred to in English as "Peter the Roman." Some have also called him Peter II.

Malachy's list was written in Latin. Here is what he wrote about the last pope on his list:

> *In persecutione extrema SRE sedebit. Petrus Romanus, quipascet oves in multis tribulationibus: quibus transactis civitas septicollis diruetur, et Iudex tremendus iudicabit populum suum. Finis.*[119]

Here an English translation from *The Catholic Encyclopedia*:

"In the final persecution of the Holy Roman Church there will reign Peter the Roman, who will feed his flock amid many tribulations, after which the seven-hilled city will be destroyed and the dreadful Judge will judge the people. The End."[120]

Here is a slightly different version of it (with the word "Rome" inserted by Catholic Priest Culleton):

St. Malachy (12th century): During the persecution of the Holy Roman Church, there will sit upon the throne, Peter the Roman...the City of Seven Hills (Rome) will be utterly destroyed and the awful Judge will then judge the people.[121]

Notice that the final Pope sits on the City of Seven Hills (which the Roman Catholic writer G. Culleton labeled Rome above), obviously the same one that Babylon the Great sits on in Revelation 17:9 (more on the similarities of the Peter the Roman prophecy and Revelation 17 are covered in chapter 5) , that God has destroyed in verses 14-18.

Here is some of what Catholic writer A. Gurugé wrote about the Peter the Roman matter:

There are many, around the world, who, thanks to this prophecy, are totally convinced that the next pope will indeed call himself 'Peter'–most not considering or caring what the implications of this could be.

In the considered opinion of the author, it is highly improbable that the next pope will be 'Petrus Romanus' or even 'Petrus II.'

For a start, given the Last Judgment implications, many respected Catholic sources have tried to point out, for quite a long time, that the pope talked about in motto 112 does not have to necessarily be the pope who follows the one described by motto 111; this 111th pope now being the current pope, Benedict XVI (#266). The justification for this "hedging' is that the mottos were not numbered in de Wyon's 1595 Lignum Vitae. The numbering, to facilitate manageability, came later. Consequently, it can be contented that the author of this prophecy, whoever it was, did not necessarily mean that the pope described in the last motto would come immediately after the one identified in the previous motto. Basically, the last, very long, atypical motto describes the last pope. This last pope may come to be at a much later time— with an indeterminate number of intervening popes between him and the one described by motto 111. Therefore, this last motto may not actually apply to the next pope, in which case, the expectation of 'Petrus Romanus' becomes mute.

But what the proponents of the 'Petrus Romanus' belief do not appear to appreciate is that the next pope, by the sheer necessity of the duties confronting him, is not going to be naive. Naiveté…is not a characteristic that one readily associates with today's cardinals. They know the ways of the world and are world politic. There will be none amongst them who is not familiar with the Malachy prophecy. They all understand what the ramifications would be if the next pope surprised them all by stating that he will be called *'Petrus Secundus.'*

The protodeacon announcing *'Petrus Secundus'* from the balcony of St. Peter's would be worse than shouting 'fire' in a crowded theater. There would be mayhem in what is likely to be another jam-packed St. Peter's Square. People would panic. There could be a stampede, people could get hurt. The authorities in Rome and the Italian government would be forced to take immediate action to quell the understandable alarm. It would be considered, quite rightly, a security threat! For the first time in over a century there could be troops, Italian, NATO or both, surrounding the Vatican. There would be no celebrations, The *Urbi et Orbi* blessing, if it was to take place, would be viewed with understandable askance.

It is difficult to imagine the next pope doing anything this reckless. It is difficult to envision the cardinal electors permitting him to do anything this reckless. Hence, it is extremely unlikely that the next pope will be *'Petrus Secundus,'* let alone *'Petrus Romanus.'* If he is, head for the hills, and hope for the best.[122]

On August 18, 2012, in a news post, I wrote the following about the above:

> Now, I agree that the next pope (who could be the last pope) may not chose the name Peter II or anything similar–but that does not mean that he could not fulfill that prophecy. It needs to be clear, whether he does or {does} not pick that name, the last pope will be a destructive antipope. Malachy's list generally did not name pontiffs, but give descriptions. And while some have concluded that Petrus Romanus is a name, it could instead be a description. The description could signify that he is a pebble (or "rocky" which is what the term *petrus* signifies) supporting the final Roman empire.[123]

So the choice to be known as Pope Francis I did not contradict my previous position that the post after Benedict XVI did not need to include the name Peter to possibly be the last pope.

The fact that he is now in Rome/Vatican City and has Italian heritage qualifies him to be a Roman (in at least some sense of the word). Also, since the Bible describes "clay" (pulverized rock) as part of the end time empire that God will destroy per Daniel 11:41-44, in that sense Pope Francis could be considered "Peter the Roman, " but again, just because he followed Pope Benedict XVI does not mean he must be the one that Malachy was referring to.

Cathedra Petri and Peter the Roman

Back in the late 1980s, my wife and I made our first trip to Saint Peter's Basilica in Vatican City.

Inside Saint Peter's, we saw what has been called the *Cathedra Petri*. This particular chair/throne has various legends attached to it. This throne is black and the bottom of its legs are about 5 feet off of the ground.

Cathedra Petri (Joyce Thiel)

The tour guide we had said that that there was a tradition/legend (which possibly can be tied to one interpretation of the 12th century Malachy prophecy) that the final pope would sit on this throne.

Allegedly, no one has sat on it since it was finished in the manner it is now displayed (or so we were told in the late 1980s). It allegedly has a board from a seat that some claim the Apostle Peter sat on underneath its black exterior (in the 17th century, Gianlorenzo Bernini worked on it to get it looking like its present form). Supposedly the last Peter, Peter the Roman, will be the one who is supposed to sit on this throne at the end.

It is also my recollection that there was a legend that the *Cathedra Petri* would move closer to the ground for a pope, one influenced by a demon, and/or a demon, like Satan to sit on it.

If Pope Francis I or someone else sits on the *Cathedra Petri* and, especially if something unusual happens near the time that happens, this would tend to give some credence to some of the legends. But, while the last pope could sit on the *Cathedra Petri*, this is not a biblical requirement.

Views of Peter the Roman

The last pope on the Malachy list has the longest description associated with him, giving rise to many concerns and questions. This has given many people reasons to wonder about the last pontiff on his list. Some have been concerned that Malachy's final word (*Finis* in Latin) means that this pontiff somehow causes the end of the world.

Some Catholic writers, who accept the Malachy prophecies, believe that Peter the Roman may personally be a problem. Others (who also accept the Malachy prophecies) see him as a prophesied faithful leader. While that latter view seems to be the opinion of others, I would again state that this differs from what I see written in the Bible (presuming that he and the last pope/antipope are the same person).

There are certain similarities between the Malachy prophecy and the Bible depending upon how both are understood, but the biblical leaning shows that an other-than-true Christian leader will likely be the last pope. Similarities of the Malachy prophecy for Peter the Roman and Revelation 17 are in the next chapter.

5. A Comparison of the Final Malachy Prophecy and Revelation 17

As mentioned earlier, there seem to be several similarities between the prophecy of Bishop Malachy and the last pope and statements in the chapter 17 of the Book of Revelation (also known as the Apocalypse).

First, let us look at the entire prediction of the final pope by Bishop Malachy as reported in *The Catholic Encyclopedia* again:

> "In the final persecution of the Holy Roman Church there will reign Peter the Roman, who will feed his flock amid many tribulations, after which the seven-hilled city will be destroyed and the dreadful Judge will judge the people. The End."[124]

Now let us notice that the Bible warns about something happening in the end time that is consistent with parts of the Malachy prophecy.

> 1 And there came one of the seven angels, who had the seven vials, and spoke with me, saying: Come, I will shew thee the condemnation of the great harlot, who sitteth upon many waters, 2 With whom the kings of the earth have committed fornication; and they who inhabit the earth, have been made drunk with the whine of her whoredom.

3 And he took me away in spirit into the desert. And I saw a woman sitting upon a scarlet coloured beast, full of names of blasphemy, having seven heads and ten horns. 4 And the woman was clothed round about with purple and scarlet, and gilt with gold, and precious stones and pearls, having a golden cup in her hand, full of the abomination and filthiness of her fornication. 5 And on her forehead a name was written: A mystery; Babylon the great, the mother of the fornications, and the abominations of the earth. 6 And I saw the woman drunk with the blood of the saints, and with the blood of the martyrs of Jesus. And I wondered, when I had seen her, with great admiration.

7 And the angel said to me: Why dost thou wonder? I will tell thee the mystery of the woman, and of the beast which carrieth her, which hath the seven heads and ten horns. 8 The beast, which thou sawest, was, and is not, and shall come up out of the bottomless pit, and go into destruction: and the inhabitants on the earth (whose names are not written in the book of life from the foundation of the world) shall wonder, seeing the beast that was, and is not.

9 And here is the understanding that hath wisdom. The seven heads are seven mountains, upon which the woman sitteth, and they are seven kings: 10 Five are fallen, one is, and the other is not yet come: and when he is

come, he must remain a short time. 11 And the beast which was, and is not: the same also is the eighth, and is of the seven, and goeth into destruction.

12 And the ten horns which thou sawest, are ten kings, who have not yet received a kingdom, but shall receive power as kings one hour after the beast. 13 These have one design: and their strength and power they shall deliver to the beast. 14 These shall fight with the Lamb, and the Lamb shall overcome them, because he is Lord of lords, and King of kings, and they that are with him are called, and elect, and faithful.

15 And he said to me: The waters which thou sawest, where the harlot sitteth, are peoples, and nations, and tongues. 16 And the ten horns which thou sawest in the beast: these shall hate the harlot, and shall make her desolate and naked, and shall eat her flesh, and shall burn her with fire. 17 For God hath given into their hearts to do that which pleaseth him: that they give their kingdom to the beast, till the words of God be fulfilled.

18 And the woman which thou sawest, is the great city, which hath kingdom over the kings of the earth. (Revelation 17:1-18, DRB)

In both Malachy's list and the Book of Revelation we see:

1. Reference to the city of seven hills/mountains.
2. The destruction of the city of seven hills/mountains.
3. The end of a power in Rome.
4. Persecution.
5. Troubles/tribulations on the earth.
6. A type of judgment.
7. Events for the end time.

The persecution that the Bible tells of is of the truly faithful (Revelation 17:6 and seemingly others per 17:16-17). And the judgment that the Bible shows happens, will also come from God (Revelation 17:1,14; cf. 6:10; 18:10).

Whether or not Pope Francis I is the last pope, the fact is that the last pope on the Malachy list seems to be very much like someone warned against in the Holy Bible.

6. What Does the Bible Teach About the Antichrist?

Other chapters in this book have referred to the fact that Catholic and biblical sources seem to point to the last pope as the final Antichrist.

To establish some of the biblical basis for this, this chapter will include quotes of all the prophecies in sacred scripture that use the term antichrist or antichrists.

The terms 'antichrist' and 'antichrists' are only used in the Bible five times (four and one respectively), and are only found in four verses of the Bible — all written by the Apostle John.

Those verses are II John 7, I John 2:18, I John 2:22, and I John 4:3. As all of them discuss some aspect of theology, they suggest that the final Antichrist is mainly a religious figure.

The Four Verses

As there are four verses that specifically mention "antichrist," let's examine all the "antichrist" verses, starting with II John:

> ⁷ For many deceivers have gone out into the world who do not confess Jesus Christ as coming in the flesh. This is a deceiver and an antichrist (II John 7).

This scripture says that antichrist is a deceiver who does "not confess Jesus Christ as coming in the flesh."

Was John trying to say that "spirit of Antichrist" is not acknowledging that there was a person named Jesus?

This seems highly unlikely, as even most atheists acknowledge there was one referred to as Jesus Christ who lived in the flesh. Thus, the last pope, whether or not he is Pope Francis I, will at least publicly acknowledge Jesus.

This spirit of Antichrist might have something to do with not actually believing a member of the Godhead actually emptied Himself of His divinity to become human (even though that is what happened according to Philippians 2:6–7) and/or not humbling oneself to truly accept Christ to live His life in their flesh. But, another view of "coming in the flesh" may be the denying that Jesus will return to the earth and remove the final pontiff, which Revelation 19:11-20 shows He will do.

John also wrote:

> 1 Beloved, do not believe every spirit, but test the spirits, whether they are of God; because many **false prophets** have gone out into the world. 2 By this you know the Spirit of God: Every spirit that confesses that Jesus Christ has come in the flesh is of God, and every spirit that does not confess that Jesus Christ has come in the flesh is not of God. 3 And this is the

spirit of the **Antichrist**, which you have heard was coming, and is now already in the world (I John 4:1-3).

This scripture similarly states that the "spirit of Antichrist" is not truly confessing that Jesus Christ has come in the flesh. It also shows that apparently some of Antichrist's teachings began when John was still alive.

These verses specifically tie in the idea that false prophets have the spirit of Antichrist. Thus, it would seem consistent with these passages to conclude that the final Antichrist would be a false prophet (which is a term that the same Apostle John uses later in the Book of Revelation).

In addition, John also wrote:

> [18] Little children, it is the last hour; and as you have heard that the Antichrist is coming, even now many antichrists have come, by which we know that it is the last hour. [19] They went out from us, but they were not of us; for if they had been of us, they would have continued with us; but they went out that they might be made manifest, that none of them were of us. [20] But you have an anointing from the Holy One, and you know all things. [21] I have not written to you because you do not know the truth, but because you know it, and that no lie is of the truth. [22] Who is a liar but he who denies that Jesus is the Christ? He is antichrist who denies the Father and the Son (I John 2:18-22).

These scriptures show that while there will be a final Antichrist, even since John's time, there have been pretended believers. These passages also state that if people were true believers, they would have continued with John's practices.

Thus, because the truly faithful Christians have continued with the practices of the Apostle John (like Passover), there is reason to believe that at the end, the final Antichrist will embrace some type of religion that is somehow against those faithful Christians who hold to some of John's practices.

Who is the Antichrist?

The first Beast, also known as 666, is not the Antichrist, because the first Beast of Revelation 13 is not mainly a religious leader.

The second beast in Revelation 13 is primarily a religious leader (even though he has political influence). He promotes religious worship and is also referred to in other scriptures as "the false prophet" (Revelation 16:13; 19:20; 20:10). He is likely to be considered a current or future saint by his followers.

It is he who is the final "Antichrist," as all the specific warnings mentioning "antichrist" in the Bible are discussing religious leaders.

The final Antichrist would also appear to be the one warned about as the antipope in various Catholic and Orthodox writings. Also, notice the following:

Priest Herman Kramer (20th century): This false prophet possibly...usurps the papal supremacy...His assumed spiritual authority and supremacy over the Church would make him resemble the Bishop of Rome...He would be Pontifex Maximus, a title of pagan emperors, having spiritual and temporal authority. Assuming authority without having it makes him the False Prophet...**Though he poses as a lamb, his doctrines betray him...**His principles and dogmas to be accepted...**it will comprise emperor-worship**...with the persecution of true believers.[125]

Priest A. Maas (20th century): Nearly all commentators find Antichrist mentioned in the Apocalypse... many scholars identify Antichrist with the beast which had "two horns, like a lamb" and spoke "as a dragon"... the Abbot really believes that Antichrist will overthrow the Pope and usurp his See...[126]

Helen Tzima Otto (2000): The anti-pope – Episcopal of the Beast, alias the false prophet...[127]

St. Hildegard (died 1179): *But now you see her from the waist down;* for you see her in her full dignity as the Church...*And from her waist to the place that denotes the female, she has various scaly blemishes... ... And thus in the place where the female is recognized is a black and monstrous head.* For the son of perdition will come raging with the arts he first used to seduce...causing people to deny God and tainting their minds and tearing the Church with the greed of rapine.[128]

Comment by Barbara Newman (1998): But as early as Scivias, Hildegard shockingly portrayed Ecclesia {the Catholic Church} as giving birth to Antichrist himself...Some other early works of Hildegard's, written before 1159, show a similar sourness of tone with respect to the institutional church.[129]

Furthermore, notice that the commentators of the *Rheims New Testament* seem to agree with my assessment:

Antichrist, if he ever were of or in the Church, shall be an Apostate and a renegade out of the Church, and he shall usurp upon it by tyranny, and by challenging worship, religion, and government thereof, so that himself shall be adored in all the Churches of the world which he list to leave standing for his honor. And this is to sit in the temple or against the Temple of God, as some interpret. If any Pope did ever this, or shall do, then let the Adversaries call him Antichrist.[130]

Thus, from biblical and other perspectives, it appears that the False Prophet/final Antichrist may be a future demon-influenced "pope."

The final Antichrist is likely to be one who changes — though he does not clearly seem to be changing (at first as he will turn against it later)-- the "Catholic" religion. It seems that this is the individual who has been warned against in both biblical and private Catholic prophecies.

The Bible Identifies that the Antichrist Will Perform Signs and Lying Wonders

In the final end times, the Bible shows that there will be signs and lying wonders. These signs will be performed by the False Prophet and some may also appear to be performed by the Beast of the Sea of Revelation 13:1-9 (cf. Daniel 8:24).

Notice some passages that many theologians (Catholic or otherwise) believe are related to the final Antichrist:

> 8 And then the lawless one will be revealed, whom the Lord will consume with the breath of His mouth and destroy with the brightness of His coming. 9 The coming of the lawless one is according to the working of Satan, with all power, signs, and lying wonders, 10 and with all unrighteous deception among those who perish, because they did not receive the love of the truth, that they might be saved. 11 And for this reason God will send them strong delusion, that they should believe the lie, 12 that they all may be condemned who did not believe the truth but had pleasure in unrighteousness. (2 Thessalonians 2:8-12)
>
> 11 Then I saw another beast coming up out of the earth, and he had two horns like a lamb and spoke like a dragon. 12 And he exercises

all the authority of the first beast in his presence, and causes the earth and those who dwell in it to worship the first beast, whose deadly wound was healed. 13 He performs great signs, so that he even makes fire come down from heaven on the earth in the sight of men. 14 And he deceives those who dwell on the earth by those signs which he was granted to do in the sight of the beast, telling those who dwell on the earth to make an image to the beast who was wounded by the sword and lived. 15 He was granted power to give breath to the image of the beast, that the image of the beast should both speak and cause as many as would not worship the image of the beast to be killed. 16 He causes all, both small and great, rich and poor, free and slave, to receive a mark on their right hand or on their foreheads, 17 and that no one may buy or sell except one who has the mark or the name of the beast, or the number of his name. (Revelation 13:11-17)

If Pope Francis I does not perform signs and wonders and never calls fire down from heaven, then he is not the final Antichrist and would not be the last Pontifex Maximus. But if he does those signs and wonders, that would pretty much guarantee that he is the final Antichrist.

Certain Private Prophecies May Mislead Catholics

The Bible warns of an end time religious leader with ties to the city of seven hills/mountains performing signs and lying wonders (Revelation 13:11-15; 2

Thessalonians 2:9-10; the Bible does, however, endorse two witnesses who will perform signs in Revelation 11:4-6). Certain private prophecies seem to look forward to an end time pontiff who performs signs/wonders or prodigies/miracles associated with end-time Bablyon.

But before we get to them, realize that Catholic writers also do realize that the warned against Babylon in Revelation is often referring to Rome. Notice the following Catholic comments on Revelation Chapter 17 from *The Original And True Rheims New Testament Of Anno Domini 1582*:

> *Annotations*...Rome...Then was it Babylon, when St. John wrote this, and then was Nero and the rest figures of Antichrist, and that city the resemblance of the principal place (wheresoever it be) that Antichrist shall reign in, about the later end of the world... The Church in Rome was one thing, and Babylon in Rome another thing.[131]

Yet, some fail to make the connection that the Bible says that a miracle-performing False Prophet and the Beast are supportive of Mystery, Babylon the Great at the end (Revelation 16:13-14). Some apparently are looking forward to a Great Monarch to work with a miracle-performing ecumenical pontiff of Rome in "Babylon."

But why would "faithful Catholics" follow someone who would change their religion?

Probably because of signs and lying wonders (cf. Matthew 24:24-25; Mark 13:22; 2 Thessalonians 2:9; Revelation 13:13-15; 16:13-14; 19:20).

We need to understand that the Bible specifically warns that it was by "sorcery all the nations were deceived" (Revelation 18:23; cf. Nahum 3:4) by that Babylonian-associated power. Sacred scripture also warns:

> 9 The coming of the lawless one is according to the working of Satan, with all power, signs, and lying wonders (2 Thessalonians 2:9).

Sadly, some Orthodox and Roman Catholics expect signs and wonders will announce the Great Monarch. Here is a prophecy from an Orthodox source:

> *Anonymou Paraphrasis* (10th century): The one true King...is destined to become manifest [be revealed]...by means...of signs...The King will hear the voice and instructions by an Angel appearing to him...he has foresight and is cognizant of the text of the prophecies...the name of the King is hidden [concealed] among the nations...And the particular manner of the king's manifestation to the public [to the world] will take place as follows: A star will appear for three days long and during the third hour of the night, on the eve of the feast day of the Mother of the Most High...And a herald speaking with a very loud voice in the course of the three days will summon and unveil the hoped for one...There will become

visible in the sky a 'nebulous firmament of the sun'…under that image will be suspended a cross…And the invisible herald from Heaven with his thunderous voice will say to the people: Is this man agreeable to you? At that moment everybody will be taken by fear and terror.[132]

Orthodox scholar H. Tzima Otto believes that the cross referred to will be red, because other signs in the sky, like a comet, will also be present.[133] And this Great Monarch is reported in other private prophecies to have a pontiff who does miracles.

There was also a prophecy by one claiming to have seen an apparition of Mary that may tie in to all of this:

> *Brother David Lopez* (August 1987): Before the great tribulation, there is going to be a sign. **We will see in the sky one great red cross** on a day of blue sky without clouds…[134]

Thus, there are sources that suggest that a cross (perhaps a red one) will be a "sign." If this happens many will sadly be deceived.

Here are some Roman Catholic prophecies that indicate that a pope and the Great Monarch will be accompanied with, and also perform, some type of miracles:

> *Bl. Anna-Maria Taigi* (19th century): After the three days of darkness, St. Peter and St. Paul,

having come down from Heaven, will preach in the whole world and designate a new Pope. A great light will flash from their bodies and will settle upon the cardinal who is to become Pope. Christianity, then, will spread throughout the world. He is the Holy Pontiff, chosen by God to withstand the storm. At the end, **he will have the gift of miracles**, and his name shall be praised over the whole earth.[135]

Abbe Souffrand (died 1828): The Great Ruler will perform such great and noble deeds that the infidels will be forced to admit the working of God's Providence. Under this reign the greatest righteousness will be practiced and the earth will bear in overabundance...[136]

St. Thomas a'Becket (12th Century): A knight shall come from the West. He shall capture Milan, Lombardy, and the three Crowns. He shall then sail to Cyprus and Famagoste and land at Jaffa, and reach Christ's grave where he will fight. **Wars and wonders shall befall till the people believe in Christ toward the end of the world.**[137]

The parallels to the ten-horned Beast and the False Prophet are undeniable (see also 2 Thessalonians 2:9-12; Revelation 18:23). But there is another one of interest. Although the Beast will reign for 3½ years from the time beginning in Daniel 11:31, since his reign starts shortly before that (precisely how long is not completely clear in the Bible), he may reign for about four or so years. Notice the similarities in the following Catholic prophecy:

> *Monk Hilarion* (died 1476): Before the Christian churches are renovated and united, God will send the Eagle (Great Monarch) who will travel to Rome and bring much happiness and good. The Holy Man (Angelic Pastor?) will bring peace between the clergy and the Eagle and his reign will last for four years.[138]

The words in ( ) were added by Priest Culleton. Other Catholic writers teach that "the Eagle" is the Great Monarch.[139] Thus, it appears that both Catholic prophecies and the Bible are foretelling of two leaders that will have power for about the same time and dominate the world. The Bible, however, warns against two that it describes just like them (Revelation 13). And also says that the Beast's reign will be short:

> 10 And when he comes, he must continue a short time (Revelation 17:10).

But, unlike the Beast of the Sea (the "he" mentioned above), the Bible does not make a similar statement about the Beast of the Earth. So, if Pope Francis I is the last pope, either the Catholic private prophecy about a four-year reign is wrong or it is meant to describe the time that both reign at the same time or a time after certain other events occur.

Because of the wars, economic pressure, persecutions, and wonders, many will be deceived into accepting the religion and economic system of the Beast and the

False Prophet (Revelation 13). Sadly, this will include many Protestants, Orthodox, Romans, agnostics, various Asian faiths, and others. Notice that Germany, initially, will apparently believe this the most according to a Roman Catholic source:

> *Bl. Johannes Amadeus de Sylva* (died 1482): In the latter days...Germany and Spain will unite under a great prince designated by God. After much slaughtering, the other nations will be forced to come into this union. There is no hope for unbelievers until all Germany becomes converted; then all happens quickly...the time will be prolonged until all countries unite under the Great Ruler. After this union mass conversions will take place...peace and prosperity will follow.[140]

Part of why this will occur is because Roman Catholics, Eastern Orthodox, and most Protestants simply do not realize that true Christianity was from the beginning and will, until the end of the Church age, be opposed to participation in carnal warfare (see also chapter 18). Because nearly all who profess Christ do not really understand what happened to the true Church in the second through fourth centuries (and beyond), their foundation appears to be "sand" and thus their combined house shall fall greatly (cf. Matthew 7:26-27).

Now, not all Catholic private prophetic writings endorse the arrival of a religious leader who performs signs and wonders. In addition to others elsewhere in this book, notice also the following from *The Catholic Encyclopedia*:

> C. *Van Den Biesen* (20th century): The beast from the land has two horns like a ram. Its power lies in its art of deceiving by means of tokens and miracles. Throughout the remainder of the book it is called the false prophet. Its office is to assist the beast from the sea, and to induce men to adore its image.[141]

Now, I agree with *The Catholic Encyclopedia* that the two-horned beast of Revelation 13:11-16 is the "false prophet" of Revelation and he will deceive people with miraculous signs. We all should be concerned if Pope Francis I or some possibly other pontiff starts performing "miracles."

A Catholic saint centuries earlier taught:

> *Saint Zenobius* (died 285): Antichrist will work a thousand prodigies on earth.[142]

And that is basically true (although the number of miracles/prodigies is not stated in scripture). Thus, Catholics and others need to be concerned about any pontiff who starts performing what will tend to be seen as multiple miracles.

Yet, notice that others seem to encourage this:

> *Abbott Joachim* (died 1202): A remarkable Pope will be seated on the pontifical throne, under special protection of the angels...he shall recover the states of the Church, and reunite

the exiled temporal powers. As the only Pastor, he shall reunite the Eastern to the Western Church...Through him the East and West shall be in ever lasting concord. The city of Babylon shall then be the head and guide of the world...At the beginning, in order to bring these happy results, having need of a powerful assistance, this holy Pontiff will ask the cooperation of the generous monarch of France (Great Monarch)...A man of remarkable sanctity will be his successor in the **Pontifical chair. Through him God will work so many prodigies that all men shall revere him**. [143]

Even though the Bible warns against end time Babylon (cf. Revelation 18:4; Jeremiah 50,51), Abbot Joachim is trying to teach that it is good. Now, if there is only one pope left as the Malachy prophecies suggest, then the above is wrong on at least that point (it requires at least one pontiff past Pope Francis I). Although some Catholics have distanced themselves from Abbot Joachim (he has sometimes been referred to as "Merlin"), the reality is that many will embrace a pontiff who performs miracles.

Current Catholics and the Final Antichrist.

There is one point that should be made clear at this stage. When this book is referring to the future "Catholic" religion, it is not saying that all who are now Catholics are currently supportive of the final religion of the final Beast.

To the contrary, I believe that most Catholics, if they truly understood it, would oppose it, as well as other changes they have adopted to alter the original faith. Actually, that was my original motivation for this book. After a visit to Vatican City some years back, I prayed about how I could help warn Catholics (later adding everyone else) about those "things which must shortly take place" (Revelation 1:1).

About four years ago, I wrote:

> I also want to make it clear that I do not believe that Pope Benedict XVI is the final prophesied Antichrist any more than Martin Luther was. Nor unless some bizarre supernatural event occurs, will Pope Benedict XVI become the final Antichrist.

The Antichrist, along with the Beast of Revelation, will change the current Catholic faith into a persecuting ecumenical form that many, including most non-Catholics, will sadly follow.

There will, however, be a great multitude of people of all backgrounds that will decide to follow the teachings of the "secret sect" that the Beast and the Antichrist will warn against:

> [9] After these things I looked, and behold, a great multitude which no one could number, of all nations, tribes, peoples, and tongues, standing before the throne and before the Lamb, clothed with white robes, with palm branches in their hands, [10] and crying out with

a loud voice, saying, "Salvation belongs to our God who sits on the throne, and to the Lamb!" (Revelation 7:9-10).

And it is my hope and prayer that this book will be one influence in encouraging every person in the world, irrespective of their current religious affiliation (or lack thereof), to at some time (now would be good) support the work of God as advocated by the most faithful Christians, and not follow the final Antichrist.

The Mystery of Lawlessness

The Antichrist is associated with lawlessness. But if this is a pope, how could that be? While there are many likely explanations, looking at sacred scripture gives several clues.

First, here is a writing from the Apostle Paul:

> 7 For the mystery of lawlessness is already at work; (2 Thessalonians 2:7)

The above shows that lawlessness was already affecting the early church. This could be a reference to people such as Simon Magus (who was condemned by the Apostle Peter in the Book of Acts 8:20-23).

Historical records show that although he claimed to be a Christian, Simon Magus and his followers were condemned by those now considered to have been early supporters of the Church of Rome (such as Justin,[144] Tertullian,[145] Irenaeus,[146] and Hippolytus[147]) for lawless doctrines such as using statues for worship, revering a woman, incantations, mysteries, mystic priests, claiming divine titles for leaders, accepting money for religious favors, preferring allegory and tradition over many aspects of scripture, divorcing from Christianity biblical practices considered to be Jewish, and having a leader who wanted to be thought of as God/Christ on Earth.

Notice the following written by the Apostle John:

5 And on her forehead a name was written:

MYSTERY, BABYLON THE GREAT, THE MOTHER OF HARLOTS AND OF THE ABOMINATIONS OF THE EARTH. (Revelation 17:5)

The above Mystery Babylon is identified as the city of seven hills/mountains (Rome) in Revelation 17:9,18.

In both the Apostle Paul's and the Apostle John's account we see not just straight lawlessness/abominations, but that there is apparently something mysterious enough about it, that this is at least part of what causes people to believe the lie (2 Thessalonians 2:9-12).

How could this apply to the last pope? Well, there are many ways, but here is another one for readers to consider. While the Protestant world tends to consider that Jesus condemned the Pharisees of His day for legalism, scripture shows a side that Protestants and various others have often missed.

Jesus condemned the Pharisees for lawlessness, hypocrisy, and holding to their traditions above the Bible:

> 27 "Woe to you, scribes and Pharisees, hypocrites! For you are like whitewashed tombs which indeed appear beautiful outwardly, but inside are full of dead men's bones and all uncleanness. 28 Even so you also outwardly appear righteous to men, but inside you are full of hypocrisy and lawlessness. (Matthew 23:27-28, NKJV)

> 1. THEN came to him from Jerusalem Scribes and Pharisees, saying, 2. Why do thy Disciples transgress the tradition of the Ancients? For they wash not their hands when they eat bread.

> 3. But he answering said to them: Why do you also transgress the commandment of God for your tradition? 4. For God said, *Honour father and mother. and, He that shall curse father or mother, dying let him die.* 5. But you say, Whosoever shall say to father or mother, The gift whatsoever proceedeth from me, shall profit thee: 6. And shall not honour his father or his mother: and you have made frustrate the commandment of God for your own tradition. 7. Hypocrites, well hath Esay prophesied of you, saying, 8. *This people honoreth me with their lips: but their heart is far from me. 9. And in vain*

do they worship me, teaching doctrines and
commandments of men. (Matthew 15:1-9, DRB)

While some tend to believe that the Pharisees kept law, the Bible shows that they violated, for example, all of the Ten Commandments.[148] They had a certain knowledge of the law, but did not properly keep it as Jesus made clear.

Even more so than the Pharisees, undoubtedly the last pope will be filled with lawlessness, hypocrisy, and holding to non-biblical traditions above the Bible while attempting to project the appearance of beauty. Because he, and those who support him, do not truly place the word of God as the top authority in their lives, he will be a promoter of lawlessness.

Jesus often called the Pharisees hypocrites (Matthew 15:7; 16:3; 22:18; 23:23,25,27,29; Mark 7:6). According to *Strong's Exhaustive Concordance,* the Greek word Jesus used that was translated as hypocrite means, "an actor under an assumed role." The final Antichrist will be like that (cf. Revelation 16:13).

Now not all the individual Pharisees were bad. Some tried to learn from Jesus (John 3:1-4). Some even tried to help Jesus (Luke 13:31). They were never condemned for that. Actually some finally did believe (Acts 15:5). Paul and Nicodemus are probably the two most famous believing Pharisees (John 3:1; Acts 23:6). Most though, could not see their sins and would not repent (Luke 18:10-14; Matthew 3:7-9; 5:20; 7:30). Remember, Jesus condemned them for pretending to keep the law and for actually breaking it (Mat 23:28).

Lest anyone feel that this condemnation of the Pharisees is in error, notice that there are some prophecies in Jeremiah that essentially confirm this:

> 8 "Behold, you trust in lying words that cannot profit. 9 Will you steal, murder, commit adultery, swear falsely, burn incense to Baal, and walk after other gods whom you do not know, 10 and then come and stand before Me in this house which is called by My name, and say, 'We are delivered to do all these abominations'? 11 Has this house, which is called by My name, become a den of thieves in your eyes? Behold, I, even I, have seen it," says the Lord. (Jeremiah 7:8-11)

> 8 "How can you say, 'We are wise, And the law of the Lord is with us'? Look, the false pen of the scribe certainly works falsehood. 9 The wise men are ashamed, They are dismayed and taken. Behold, they have rejected the word of the Lord; So what wisdom do they have? (Jeremiah 8:8-9)

Hence, there will be leaders and people who claimed to have true religion, yet were violating the Ten Commandments. Thus, apparently some of the Pharisees, to a degree, fulfilled this prophecy, as will certain supporters of the last pope.

The Apostle Paul also warned that Satan's ministers would appear to be good, but would not be:

10. The truth of Christ is in me, that this glorying shall not be infringed toward me in the countries of Achaia. 11. Wherefore? because I love you not? God doth know. 12. But that which I do, I will also do, that I may cut away the occasion of them that desire occasion: that, in that which they glory, they may be found men like us. 13. For such false apostles are crafty workers, transfiguring themselves into Apostles of Christ.

14. And no marvel: for Satan himself transfigureth himself into an Angel of light. 15. It is not great matter therefore if his ministers be transfigured as the ministers of justice: whose end shall be according to their works. (II Corintians 11:10-15, DRB)

The last pope will not be good and his reign will not end well.

He will subtly promote lawlessness. Yet, because of signs, lying wonders, preferences among many for traditions over the truth of God, the vast majority of humans will be deceived and the world will get to the point of near total destruction. It will only be because of the intervention of God and the return of Jesus Christ that all will not perish (Matthew 24:23,30).

Satanic deception will be the legacy of the final Antichrist. The one I who will apparently be the last pope.

7. Is the Pope Catholic or Will He Betray Rome?

In some households, the expression, "Is the Pope Catholic?," is asked with the intent of suggesting a "yes" or "obviously yes" response to a question. Since the fourth century, the popes have all claimed to be Catholic (they were not called "pontifex maximus" prior to then) and the vast majority have been Roman Catholic in their faith. Some were more hypocritical, etc. and thus this author would be hesitant to claim that all the Bishops of Rome have truly held to the faith of that church.

But is it possible that the last pope, who could be Pope Francis I, will not be Roman Catholic? On the surface this seems absurd.

As discussed in chapter 2, prior to becoming Pope Francis I, Jorge Mario Bergoglio went to Catholic seminary, became a Catholic priest, then a bishop, then a cardinal, and then on March 13, 2013, the Bishop of Rome. So, to most he clearly is a Catholic. And Pope Francis I may well truly be.

But if he is the last and final pope, then the Bible shows that he will allow compromise mightily and allow the Catholic Church of Rome to be betrayed, hence suggesting that he would not then be true to the Catholic faith.

Connecting the Dots

As cited earlier, the Bible tells of a religious leader

who will rise up and support the final European Beast power to the point of attempting to force people to worship that Beast (Revelation 13:11-17).

Although some have suggested that the ten-horned Beast of the Sea (Revelation 13:1-4) will turn against and burn the two-horned Beast of the Earth (Revelation 13:11), based upon the teachings of Revelation 17:16-17, since this two-horned Beast is the False Prophet of Revelation 16:13 and he gets burnt by Jesus and His angels (Revelation 19:15-21, someone or something else must get destroyed in Revelation 17.

The Bible specifies that the someone/something is a city that rules over the world. Since the time of Jesus, what are the only organizations that ruled over much of the old Roman Empire from a seven-hilled city?

They would include the old Roman Empire, the Church of Rome, and to a lessor degree, the Eastern Orthodox Church (Constantinople/ Istanbul is on seven-hills, similar to Rome and had a certain prominence for about 1,000 years). They have had relations with world rulers that have not always lived up to New Testament ideals and actually are the only ones that could possibly fit the historical record.

Now since parts of both Roman and Orthodox Catholic prophecy show that Rome wins out between the two in the end in terms of final top leader, this is consistent with the historical understanding within the Church of God that Rome is the unfaithful woman in Revelation 17. Presuming that is the case, then if one connects-the-dots, it is the Church of Rome that gets betrayed by supporters of the ten-horned Beast in Revelation 17. And since the two-horned Beast is a major supporter of the ten-horned Beast, he then has at least some responsibility in this end time destruction of the Church of Rome (for more dots to connect, see also chapters 5 and 12).

Since it should be almost inconceivable that a pope that was truly Roman Catholic in the sense of the *Catechism of the Catholic Church* would totally betray his church, this is why I am suggesting that the last pope will not truly be Catholic.

This destruction of Rome is consistent with various Catholic private prophecies that suggest that a top Roman clergy member (like a pope) would betray their church and oversee the destruction of Rome.

If the following private prophecy comes to pass, I suspect that the last pope, near or after he betrays the Church of Rome, will endorse it (or at least part of it):

> *Bernadine Von Busto* (died 1490): Satan...will cause a voice to come from the crucifix saying "...I am not God nor the savior but a sorcerer, an instigator and deceiver of the people...the greatest sorcerer the world has ever seen..."Also the pictures of the Mother of God at times will speak when someone will be praying before them: `Cease your supplications. I am not the Mother of God. I have no power with God. I am only a miserable creature...' It will be the same with the pictures of the Saints. That it is the devil

who speaks from the crucifixes and pictures...[149]

And if the above happens, while Satan would be telling certain truths there (he is, after all, capable of even quoting scripture per Matthew 4), he may be doing this to get people to support the final battle that is staged at Armageddon (Revelation 16:13-16) — the one that the False Prophet is involved in getting people to support. And no Christian would want to be part of this.

For years I have believed that the last pope would not truly be Catholic. He would be a different type of "antipope" (most antipopes occurred because of disputed elections, but I have suggested that a pontiff who does not hold too many of the core beliefs of the Church of Rome would also seem to fit the definition of an antipope).

Will Pope Francis I end up being that pontiff?

8. The Biblical Dangers of the Great Monarch

Certain Catholics believe that a militaristic political leader will arise, be confirmed by a pope that does miracles, and will establish a version of their faith that will be accepted by nearly all. And various Catholic and Eastern Orthodox writers suggest that this Great Monarch is sent by God.

Yet, it should be pointed out that the Catholic Great Monarch would seem to be the same person as the ten-horned Beast, also known as 666 and as the final "King of the North."

Since the focus of this book is the last pope, I will not quote most of the Great Monarch private prophecies in this book. More details, however, can be found at the www.cogwriter.com website.

But, before getting to summaries of "Great Monarch" private prophecies, here are some that make it clear that in the latter days some Catholics expect to have a future emperor of Europe, who with a major pope, will control the Earth:

> *Capuchin Friar* (18th century): A scion of the Carlovingian race {a descendant of Charlemagne}, by all considered extinct, will come to Rome to behold and admire the piety and clemency of this Pontiff, who will crown him, and declare him to be the legitimate Emperor of the Romans, and from the Chair of

St. Peter, the Pope will lift the standard, the crucifix, and will give it to the new emperor.[150]

Venerable Bartholomew Holzhauser (Born in the 17th century, in Germany): There will rise a valiant monarch anointed by God. He will be Catholic...He will rule supreme in temporal matters. The pope will rule supreme in spiritual matters at the same time.

The reign of the Great Ruler may be compared with that of Caesar Augustus...also with the reign of Emperor Constantine the Great, who was sent by God, after severe persecutions, to deliver both the Church and State. By his victories on water and land he brought the Roman empire under subjection, which he then ruled in peace...'Golden crown' refers to his Holy Roman (German) Empire...[151]

St. Ephraem (5th century): Then the Lord from his glorious heaven shall set up his peace. And the kingdom of the Romans shall rise in place of this latter people, and establish dominion upon the earth, even to its ends, and there shall be no one who will resist it.

Comment on the above from Catholic writer Desmond Birch: He is talking about some future "Kingdom of the Romans" of a "latter people."[152]

Many biblical and private prophecies tell of a future European emperor/king. Some are looking for a type of resurrected "Holy Roman Empire."

History shows that European emperors who attempt to establish dominion upon the Earth tend to do that through conquering. The next real one will apparently follow that same conquering approach, though the Bible warns that he will get in peaceably (Daniel 11:21,24; cf. 8:23-25).

The following shows that this leader is supposed to eliminate the forces of Islam:

> *Rudolph Gekner* (died 1675): **A great prince of the North with a most powerful army will traverse all Europe, uproot all republics, and exterminate all rebels**. His sword moved by Divine power will most valiantly defend the Church of Jesus Christ. He will combat on behalf of the true orthodox faith, and shall subdue to his dominion the Mahometan Empire. A new pastor of the universal church will come from the shore (of Dalmatia) through a celestial prodigy, and in simplicity of heart adorned with the doctrines of Jesus Christ. Peace will come to the world.[153]

This seems to be consistent with the King of the North taking over an Arabic power in Daniel 11:40-43.

Summary of Private Prophecies and Sacred Scripture Related to One who Sounds Like "The Great Monarch"

The following are summaries of Roman and Orthodox Catholic prophetic writings about this "Monarch" that seem to align with end time scriptures related to the final Beast power:

1. He will have Franco-German (Assyrian) ancestry (cf. Isaiah 10:5-11; Zephaniah 2:13-15).
2. He will be like a beast that could be from the sea (Revelation 13:1-2).
3. He will be announced with signs and wonders (2 Thessalonians 2:9-12; Revelation 13:13-15).
4. He will understand mysterious/sinister /futuristic things (Daniel 8:23).
5. He will be a smooth talker (Daniel 8:25; 11:23-24).
6. He will make changes, probably affecting religion (cf. Daniel 7:25; 11:37-38).
7. He, and his objectives, will be supported by "Mary" (2 Thessalonians 2:9-12).
8. He will rise up unexpectedly (Daniel 8:23-24; 11:21-24).
9. He will be considered to be a man bringing peace (Daniel 8:25; 11:21-24).
10. He will gain power after civil unrest/riots/warring in Europe (cf. Daniel 7:24; Revelation 13:3-4).
11. He will "uproot all republics" (cf. Revelation 17:12-13).

12. He will establish a new religious order while also endorsing an existing faith (cf. Daniel 11:38).
13. He will endorse certain idols/icons (Revelation 13:14-17; cf. Daniel 11:38).
14. His supporters will be identified with a sign/mark/image, like a cross and/or crucifix (cf. Revelation 13:14-17). Images of "Mary" are also expected (Isaiah 47:5,12; 2 Thessalonians 2:9-12; cf. Revelation 13:14-17).
15. He will endorse an ecumenical form of Catholicism (cf. Daniel 11:36-38; Revelation 13:3-4; 17:1-11).
16. He and a certain pope will reign about four years (cf. Daniel 7:25; 11:21-44; 12:11-12; Revelation 12:14).
17. He will establish himself militarily in Jerusalem near the beginning of his reign (Daniel 11:31; Luke 21:24).
18. He will be the leader of the resurrected (presumed dead) Holy Roman Empire (Revelation 13:3,12).
19. He will establish "New Babylon" (cf. Jeremiah 50:42; 51:33; Revelation 18:11-21).
20. He will help the Seven-Hilled city reign (cf. Revelation 17:9,18).
21. He will eliminate the English peoples, who had been strong (Daniel 11:39).
22. He will spread his form of religion around the world (Revelation 13:3-17).
23. "The Great Monarch will annihilate heretics and unbelievers" (cf. Daniel 7:25; 11:28-35; Matthew 10:23; Revelation 14:12-13).

24. During his time, "Protestantism will cease" (cf. Revelation 13:3-4,8).
25. He will divide up the lands of the English peoples (Daniel 11:39; Ezekiel 5:1-4).
26. His supporters will be opposed to those that keep the Sabbath (cf. Daniel 7:25; Revelation 12:17; Revelation 13:16-17).
27. The Anglo peoples will betray each other (Isaiah 9:19-21).
28. The world will prosper under his system for a while (Daniel 11:39; Revelation 18:9-19).
29. He will eliminate Muslims (Daniel 11:40-43; Ezekiel 30:1-9).
30. He "will amass gold" and help the world prosper with gold (Daniel 11:43; cf. Revelation 18:11-16).
31. Allegedly, "Happiness will reign in the world as it did in the days of Noah" under his leadership (cf. Matthew 24:37-38; Luke 17:26-27).
32. He will die in or near Jerusalem (cf. Revelation 16:13-16; 19:19-20).
33. His kingdom will be destroyed by the battle associated with Armageddon (Revelation 16:13-16).
34. A supposed "Antichrist" (who scripture identifies as actually Jesus) comes after his reign (Revelation 19:11-21).

Lee Penn noted:

> The tradition of the Great King and the Holy Pope...first emerged from the *Tiburtine Sibyl*, a work that may date back to AD 380-

400...expectations for a future Great Monarch and a Holy Pope are not defined in scripture or any Conciliar decrees or in any other official teaching of the Catholic Church...

Catholic writer Paul Thigpen warns, "Looking for the Great Monarch, then, who does not appear in Scripture, might lead to overlooking the Antichrist who does. It might even lead to-- a more disturbing thought--to mistaking the Antichrist for the Great Monarch. After all, lesser antichrists of the past such as Hitler and Stalin have seduced followers with visions of grand and glorious earthly kingdoms. Surely Antichrist of the last days will do the same." [154]

And even though the above confuses the title "Antichrist" with the Beast-power, the basic point is correct that the acceptance of the "Great Monarch" will result in people supporting him (the final Beast/King of the North) and the final Antichrist.

It should be mentioned that some Roman Catholic prophecies indicate these leaders, which tend to be referred to as the "Great Monarch" and Angelic Pastor," are French, while others indicate German ethnicity. There are also blatant contradictions among them. It is most likely that these leaders may have some type of blended ethnicities. Perhaps, the Beast could have been born in Germany of the Habsburg line through his mother (or father) or have an Austrian father and a French mother or some other way involving Franco-German ancestry.

Many in Pompeii Met With Unexpected Destruction
(Joyce Thiel)

There has long been a connection between the original Roman Empire and the Germans and the French. For example, there was the "Emperor of the Franks, Charlemagne (a German hero as well as a French one)" who was considered to have been Emperor of the "Holy Roman Empire."[155] Technically, Otto I the German was the first one officially crowned with that title in 962.[156] Charlemagne was crowned *Imperator Augustus* by Pope Leo III on 25 December 800.[157] The Habsburg/Hapsburg line decends through Charlemagne as have all the official emperors of the old "Holy Roman Empire."

Titles once given to the late Otto von Habsburg (who died on July 4, 2011) included "Emperor of Austria; King of Hungary and Bohemia, Dalmatia, Croatia, Slavonia, Galicia and Lodomeria; King of

Jerusalem."[158] It may be that other Habsburg relatives may also end up with those or similar titles. The "King of Jerusalem" title is of interest as the Bible warns about the King of the North going to Jerusalem (Daniel 11:31; Matthew 24:15) and Catholic prophecy indicates that their "Great Monarch" will also apparently conquer Jerusalem[159] and reign there, at least for a time.[160]

A Remergence of a European Empire

Some wish for recreation of the Roman Empire and some others wish for a reemergence of the old Holy Roman Empire. This is something that some in the European Union (EU) seems to be working towards (though the EU will need to change further to bring it about). But the EU is not the first relatively recent attempt.

Adolf Hitler declared at Nuremberg, September 12, 1938;- "The Holy Roman Empire begins to breathe again..."[161] as he felt he was to re-establish the final European empire. A cross was a symbol used by both Charlemagne and Hitler (as well as many of the Habsburgs), and Catholic prophecies suggest that it will be a symbol of the supporters of the Great Monarch.

Here are some Catholic warnings about the type of unification that some look forward to:

> *Michal Semin:* Our Lady spoke of the annihilation of nations...The European Union is intent on destroying nation states,

suppressing national identities and borders, so that we can happily live in an always progressing supra-national community of EU faithful.[162]

Priest O'Connor (20th century?): **This final false prophet will be a bishop of the church and will lead all religions into becoming one**.[163]

Priest H. Kramer (20th century): In the vision of the Seer now appears a second beast rising out of the earth, having two horns like a lamb but speaking like a dragon...In other places he is called the false prophet...This prophet may re-establish the pagan Roman Empire and build the "Great Harlot", Babylon... The False Prophet...will persuade all infidels, apostates and apostate nations to worship and adore him...Antichrist "sitteth in the temple of God" (2 Thes. II. 4). This is not the ancient Temple in Jerusalem...this temple is shown to be a Catholic Church...The False Prophet will proclaim the resurrection of the Roman Empire.[164]

Thus, while some Catholic prophecies praise a new religious order, many others indicate that a new type of "Catholicism" will be false to that religion and not be good for Europe. This also seems to be consistent with an Orthodox understanding of the last false religious power coming from Rome:

Bishop Gerasimos of Abydos (20th century): The army of Antichrist is made up of the worldly powers, mainly the Roman Empire, symbolized by the two beasts and the harlot woman (Rev. 11:7; 13:1-17; cf. Dan. 7:11-12)… The final confrontation with evil is presented in chapters 19 and 20…The war is waged by the beast and the false prophet. **Both of these are organs of Satan, representing the political and religious authority of Rome** (Rev. 13:1-18).[165]

Whatever new order that the Great Monarch (who is to be crowned the leader of the Roman Empire according to other writings) implements with Rome will not be faithful to the teachings of Christ or His original faithful followers.

Therefore a "false pope" is expected, and a great loss of Catholic members to his religion is prophesied. Might this be in the works now? Could Pope Francis I work for this?

Apparitions Claiming to Be Mary May Be Involved in the End

Although many of the Catholic prophecies show that their Great Monarch will spread a version of "Catholicism" all over the world and a pope will do miracles, it perhaps should be mentioned that others indicate that some type of Marian image/apparition will be involved in insuring his success over non-Catholics:

> *R. Gerald Culleton* (20th century): During the reign of the Great Monarch and the Angelic

Pastor the Catholic Church will spread throughout the world, conversions will be innumerable...The Blessed Virgin will be the chief one in gaining victory over all heresy and schism because of **her power over the demons in the last ages of the world will be especially great**. This will be recognized by her enthronement as "Mistress and Queen of Men's Hearts."[166]

St. Louis-Marie Grignion De Montfort (18th century): **The power of Mary over all the devils will be particularly outstanding in the last period of time**. She will extend the Kingdom of Christ over the idolaters and Moslems, and there will come glorious era when Mary is the Ruler and Queen of Hearts.[167]

St. Louis De Montfort (died 1720): The training and education of the great saints, who will appear towards the end of the world, is reserved for the Mother of God...These great saints, full of grace and zeal, will be chosen in order to oppose the enemies of God who will appear everywhere. By their word and example these saints will bring the whole world to a true veneration of Mary.[168]

Notice that this alleged "Mary" also has the power over the demons. As the Bible never indicates that the biblical Mary has this power, this is apparently a reference to a demonic manifestation/apparition claiming to be Mary. And notice that many are working for this apparition to put down those who oppose the extreme veneration of Mary.

Here is some of what the Roman Catholic academic Jean Guitton concluded in 1973 about what some of the apparitions were teaching:

> One of the themes of Grignon de Monfort is that devotion to Mary would grow toward the end of time, that the progress of this cult would be a sign of the end times.[169]

Also notice the following from Pope John Paul II:

> Christ will be victorious by means of Her, because He wishes that the victories of the Church in the contemporary world and in the future will be united to Her.[170]

The idea that "Mary" will be part of the end times is clearly within Roman Catholic literature.

Here is another Roman Catholic prophecy:

> *Anna-Katarina Emmerick* (July 12, 1820): I had a vision of the holy Emperor Henry. I saw him at night kneeling alone at the foot of the main alter in a great and beautiful church...and I saw the Blessed Virgin coming down all alone...The wine was as red as blood, and there was also some water. The Mass was short. The Gospel of St. John was not read at the end. When the Mass had ended, Mary came up to Henry (the Emperor), and she extended her right hand

towards him, saying that it was in recognition of his purity. Then, she urged him not to falter...[171]

Catholic writer Yves Dupont (20th century): Henry is the Great Monarch, chosen by God to restore all things to Christ...The Blessed Virgin urges him not to falter.[172]

Here is what another Roman Catholic wrote related to "Mary":

Blessed Mary of Agreda (17th century): It was revealed to me that through the intercession of the Mother of God all heresies will disappear. The victory over heresies had been reserved by Christ for His Blessed Mother. In the last times, the Lord will in a special manner spread the renown of His Mother: Mary began salvation, and by her intercession it will be completed. Before the second coming of Christ, Mary must, more than ever, shine in mercy, might, and grace in order to bring unbelievers into the Catholic Faith. The power of Mary in the last times over the demons will be very conspicuous. **Mary will extend the reign of Christ over the heathen and the Mohammedans**...[173]

It is interesting to note that several things attributed to Mary are the same or similar to those of the Great Monarch. Thus, perhaps the Great Monarch, or some of his followers like the last pope, will somehow claim to have seen and/or received help from "Mary."

Protestants who are starting to look more towards "Mary," may help fulfill the *Agreda* prophecy above. There is a very high probability that in the future, one or more "Marian" apparitions will become public and mislead many (cf. Isaiah 47; 2 Thessalonians 2:9-12).

If more public "Marian" appearances come to pass, then these apparitions may be one of the many signs and lying wonders (cf. 2 Thessalonians 2:9; Matthew 24:24; Mark 13:22; Revelation 16:14) and even "sorcery" (Revelation 18:23; 19:20; Isaiah 47:9,12; Nahum 3:4) that will help persuade people to support the future King of the North. The Beast, which certain Catholic prophets seem to call the Great Monarch, will then help persuade the world to accept a more ecumenical form of Catholicism.

Some improperly consider that a non-biblical version of "Mary is our hope. She is...our sign."[174] Yet, the Bible warns that a certain virgin, lady, city, mother, and harlot, all make the same type of statements as all are condemned (Isaiah 47:1-14; Zephaniah 2:15; Revelation 17:1-18; 18:7-8), despite "miraculous signs" sometimes called *sorceries* being involved — all should be careful not to fall for them or their Babylonian system.

The Bible specifically warns about a "daughter of the Chaldeans" which considers itself "the Lady of the Kingdoms" that has "children" and long had sorceries and enchantments that mislead others (Isaiah 47:5-12) that will be punished (Revelation 18:7-8). This biblically condemned "Lady of the Kingdoms" makes nearly identical statements to a particular city (Zephaniah 2:15) and a harlot who is associated with the city on seven hills/mountains (Revelation 17:1-18; 18:7).

In 1846 there was an apparition believed to be Mary in La Salette, France that has been accepted by the Vatican. Although not all parts of the message have been accepted by the Vatican, it has been claimed that a Roman Catholic priest named Parent wrote the following related to Maximin, one of the two children who claimed to see the apparition (the other child was named Melanie):

> Furthermore, each secret must contain special prophecies of a particular character. So what would be the particular mark of Maximin's secret? Principally, it would seem to proclaim the triumph of the Church and above all it would seem to designate the political saviour, referred to in so many prophecies by the popular name of the Grand Monarch.[175]

So, this would be consistent with other Catholic writers that a Great Monarch is expected, and that there may be ties to apparitions. (More details on apparitions are in my book *Fatima Shock!*[176])

Walk By Faith, Do Not Accept the 'Great Monarch' or Various Improper Signs

According to one or more Catholic writers, the Great Monarch has many similarities to the King of the North, the Beast of the Sea of Revelation 13, etc. that

111

no real Christian like him is prophesied to arise in the end times.

Instead the Bible warns against someone that sounds like him, as well as one who would tend to support him above all (Revelation 13:11-17), one who would be the Beast of the Earth (Revelation 13:11) as well as the False Prophet (Revelation 16:13), the final Antichrist (1 John 4:1-3), the apparent last pope.

No one who believes the Bible should fall for the "Great Monarch" even if he is announced with signs and wonders. 2 Thessalonians 2:7-10 warns that someone sounding like him will be followed by many, while Revelation 13:11-17 shows what seems to be the last pope performing signs and wonders on behalf of such a leader.

The "Great Monarch" and the "miraculous last pope" seem to resemble quite closely the Beast of the Sea and the Beast of the Earth that the Bible warns about. Even if you see "miracles" associated with them or from apparitions that claim to be Mary, the Bible teaches that Christians are not to look mainly to outward signs:

> 7 For we walk by faith, and not by sight. (2 Corinthians 5:7, DRB)

Those who are aware of these matters prior to the time that they happen perhaps will have enough "love of the truth" that they, unlike others, will not end up being deceived (2 Thessalonians 2:9-12).

Jesus taught that in the end, nearly everyone would be deceived (Matthew 24:24), and people should pay attention to warnings before hand as well as watch what would be happening in the end time:

22. For there shall rise up false Christs and false Prophets, and they shall show signs and wonders, to seduce (if it be possible) the elect also. 23. You therefore take heed: behold I have foretold you all things.

28. And of the figures learn ye a parable. When now the bough thereof is tender, and the leaves come forth, you know that summer is very nigh. 29. So you also when you shall see these things come to pass, know ye that it is very nigh, at the door. 30. Amen I say to you, that this generation shall not pass, until all these things be done. 31. Heaven and earth shall pass, but my words shall not pass. 32. But of that day or hour no man knoweth, neither the Angels in heaven, nor the Son, but the Father. 33. Take heed, watch, an pray for you know not when the time is.

34. Even as a man who being gone into a strange country, left his house: and gave his servants authority over each work, and commanded the porter to watch. 35. Watch ye therefore (for you know not when the lord of the house cometh: at even, or at midnight, or at the cock crowing, or in the morning.) 36. Lest coming upon asudden, he find you sleeping.

37. And that which I say to you, I say to all, Watch. (Mark 13:22-23, 28-33, DRB)

While we do not yet know "that day or hour," an antipope would seem to be one of the "false Christs" that Jesus was referring to. Despite the warnings from Jesus, in the end the Beast (who sounds like the Great Monarch), a miracle performing attending False Prophet (apparent antipope), and other wonders will be part of why nearly all would be deceived.

Will you heed Jesus' words and properly watch? Do you really have enough of the "love of the truth" that you will not be deceived when you see more of the events that the Bible will happen before your eyes in the 21st century? Even if some "miraculous" signs come from the last pope?

9. Protestant Papal Antichrist Views Have Been Changing

A historical development in the Protestant world has been a change as to who will be the final Antichrist.

While defining "Protestant" doctrines is difficult as there are many variations, if Protestants are basically defined as those whose faith came out of the highly Martin Luther influenced Protestant Reformation, then many Protestants have changed (or at least tempered) their views.

Martin Luther considered that the papacy represented Antichrist.

Notice one such comment from Martin Luther:

> The reign of the Pope is so opposed to the law of Christ and the life of the Christian, that it will be safer to roam the desert and never see the face of man, than abide under the rule of Antichrist.[177]

Furthermore, nearly all Protestants in the past have believed something similar to that. For example, notice what the 19th century Scottish religious historian and Presbyterian minister, James Aitken Wylie, most famous for writing *The History of Protestantism*, wrote:

> The Apostle John, speaking of the great apostasy to arise in Christendom, calls it the "Antichrist." And the Pope has taken to

himself, as the name that best describes his office, the title "Vicar of Christ." All we shall ask as the basis of our argument are these two accepted facts, namely, that John styles the "apostasy," "the Antichrist," and that the head of the Roman system styles himself "Christ's Vicar."

The Papacy holds in its name the key of its meaning. We shall make use of that key in unlocking its mystery and true character. The Papacy cannot complain though we adopt this line of interpretation. We do nothing more than use the key it has put into our hands.

The Apostle John, we have said, speaking of the apostasy, the coming of which he predicts, styles it the "Antichrist." And we have also said that the Papacy, speaking through its representative and head, calls itself the "Vicar of Christ." The first, "Antichrist," is a Greek word, the second, "Vicar," is an English word; but the two are in reality one, for both words have the same meaning. Antichrist translated into English is Vice- Christ, or Vicar of Christ; and Vicar of Christ, rendered into Greek is Antichrist -- Antichristos. If we can establish this, and the ordinary use of the word by those to whom the Greek was a vernacular, is decisive on the point -- we shall have no difficulty in showing that this is the meaning of the word "Antichrist," -- even a Vice-Christ. And if so, then every time the Pope claims to be the Vicar of Christ, he pleads at the bar of the world that he is the "Antichrist."[178]

However, many modern Protestant scholars, including evangelical ones, seem to be shying away from that historic Protestant teaching. For example, Dr. Walvoord wrote:

> No prophecy is mentioned in the epistles of 2 John and 3 John...
>
> {Revelation 17}(v. 10). If the hills represent kings, then they do not refer to Rome, and the whole conclusion that Rome is ecclesiastical Babylon is brought into question...
>
> Revelation...(17:18). This statement must be taken as a representative of the religious character of Babylon...possibly referring to the Vatican.[179]

That book by Dr. Walvoord claims to cover essentially all Bible prophecies, yet he never once mentioned the term "Antichrist" while covering John's epistles, which are the only places that actually use that term in the Bible. For some reason his extensive *Prophecy Knowledge Handbook* does not seem to ever discuss the term "Antichrist" or who it may be. (I read the entire book and do not recall seeing the term, nor is it in the index nor are the verses in the Bible that mention antichrist specifically discussed.) While he seems to acknowledge that the Vatican *may* be condemned in the Bible, he never once states that it or some future pontiff may be the final Antichrist. In other quotes in his book, it seems to me that he really wishes to distance himself from that teaching.

Other American Protestant scholars also seem to be leaning against teaching against the Vatican. According to E. Bynum, Billy Graham, for one prominent example, in 1948 taught against Catholicism, but a later he changed his mind:

> **In 1948,** Graham said, "The three gravest menaces faced by orthodox Christianity are communism, Roman Catholicism, and Mohammedanism," **NOW**, he is continually saying nice things about the Catholics...
>
> Billy Graham says: "Anyone who makes a decision at our meetings is referred to a local clergyman, Protestant, Catholic, or Jewish." (1957) Roman Catholic Cardinal Cushing said: "I am 100% for the evangelist . . . I have never known a religious crusade that was more effective than Dr. Graham's. I have never heard the slightest criticism of anything he has ever said from any Catholic source." (1964) In 1963 Billy Graham said that he had a Roman Catholic bishop stand beside him and bless the "converts" as they came forward in Sao Paulo, Brazil. [180]

Billy Graham did not remain a Protestant opposed to a likely final Vatican Antichrist.

As he has long worked with the Catholics, he does not publicly warn against one of them being the final Antichrist.

John Hagee, for another example, appears to have perhaps renounced his position about the Vatican being future Babylon. In 2008 as he apologized for earlier anti-Catholic comments and said he hoped to advance greater unity among Catholics and evangelicals.[181]

It would appear that anti-papal positions originated during the Smyrna and/or Pergamos eras of the Church of God and versions were later adopted by Protestants such as Martin Luther.[182] The modern Protestant softening against traditional anti-Catholic positions will likely help allow the religion of Antichrist to be accepted by more at the time of the end.

The lack of realization by many Protestants that the apparently final pontiff will be an ecumenical False Prophet and the final Antichrist will sadly result in many of them joining to support him and the Beast. Hopefully, this will be only temporary.

Due to politics and laxness, even an evangelical Protestant has indicated that his movement is doomed to decline and likely have many leave it and join the Greco-Romans:

> *Michael Spencer* (2009): We are on the verge – within 10 years – of a major collapse of evangelical Christianity. This breakdown will

follow the deterioration of the mainline Protestant world and it will fundamentally alter the religious and cultural environment in the West...Millions of Evangelicals will quit...massive majorities of Evangelicals can't articulate the Gospel with any coherence...Even in areas where Evangelicals imagine themselves strong (like the Bible Belt), we will find a great inability to pass on to our children a vital evangelical confidence in the Bible and the importance of the faith...Two of the beneficiaries will be the Roman Catholic and Orthodox communions. Evangelicals have been entering these churches in recent decades and that trend will continue, with more efforts aimed at the "conversion" of Evangelicals to the Catholic and Orthodox traditions...[183]

Once signs and lying wonders happen (2 Thessalonians 2:9; Revelation 13:13:13-15; 19:20) this departure amongst the remaining evangelicals is likely to greatly accelerate.

Many Protestants will end up following the last pope.

10. 6,000 Years: Does the Bible Teach This is the Time for the Last Pope?

There has long been a teaching that God had a 7,000 year plan with two parts. One part was that humans being were being given 6,000 years to live on their own, with their own governments, and basically cut off from God. The other part, that lasts 1,000 years, has to do with the return of Jesus Christ and the establishment of His Kingdom. This "7,000 year" teaching was based upon various scriptures and was also discussed in early writings among those who professed Christ, as well as in more modern sources.

If the 6,000 years for humans to rule before Jesus returns is almost up, could it possibly end right after (or during, depending on how the year-long "the Day of the Lord," fits in; cf. Isaiah 34:8) the pontificate of Pope Francis I? This 6,000 year teaching is another reason why Pope Francis I could be the last pope.

Truly understanding what the Bible teaches about this may be helpful to *all* in these latter days, and not only to those who base their beliefs on it.

Have People Long Believed in Six Thousand Years of Human Rule?

There is an old tradition that the prophet Elijah taught that there would be six thousand years for humans to rule under Satan's kingdom, followed by one thousand years of abundance in the kingdom of God. In the late 18th century, the historian Edward Gibbon documented certain facts regarding the first century Christians:

> The ancient and popular doctrine of the Millennium was intimately connected with the second coming of Christ. As the works of the creation had been finished in six days, their duration in their present state, according to a tradition which was attributed to the prophet Elijah, was fixed to six thousand years. By the same analogy it was inferred that this long period of labor and contention, which was now almost elapsed, would be succeeded by a joyful Sabbath of a thousand years; and that Christ, with the triumphant band of the saints and the elect who had escaped death, or who had been miraculously revived, would reign upon earth till the time appointed for the last and general resurrection.[184]

While traditions should never supersede scripture, the above is certainly an interesting and ancient tradition, as it shows that the idea of a six-thousand-year plan, followed by Christ establishing His kingdom on the Earth was a common teaching among those who professed Christ in the early days.

Here are specific Jewish traditions related to the millennium from the Talmud, Sanhedrin 97a:

> *R. Kattina* said: Six thousand years shall the world exist, and one [thousand, the seventh], it shall be desolate, as it is written, And the Lord alone shall be exalted in that day {Isaiah 2:11}.

Abaye said: it will be desolate two [thousand], as it is said, After two days will he revive us: in the third day, he will raise us up, and we shall live in his sight {Hosea 6:2}.

It has been taught in accordance with R. Kattina: Just as the seventh year is one year of release in seven, so is the world: one thousand years out of seven shall be fallow, as it is written, And the Lord alone shall be exalted in that day,' and it is further said, A Psalm and song for the Sabbath day {Psalm 92:1}, meaning the day that is altogether Sabbath — and it is also said, For a thousand years in thy sight are but as yesterday when it is past {Psalm 90:4}.

The Tanna debe Eliyyahu teaches: The world is to exist six thousand years. In the first two thousand there was desolation; two thousand years the Torah flourished; and the next two thousand years is the Messianic era.[185]

Note: I inserted the scriptures quoted or alluded to above within { }, as they are in the footnotes associated with the above.

And while there are some errors in that Talmudic understanding, it supports the idea that there is a six-thousand-year plan, that the current two thousand years essentially represents the Church/Messianic era, and that a one thousand year period remains. Apparently, according to at least one of those Jewish scholars, the 6,000 years would likely be over in the next decade or so, if Jesus was the Messiah (and, of course, He was).

Futhermore, notice the following understanding from a modern Jewish source:

> According to the Talmud (Sanhedrin 97a), history will last only 6,000 years from the time of creation. The Messiah must come prior to the 6,000-years, and bring us to the next higher spiritual reality millennium.[186]

Notice what the respected Protestant historian Johann Karl Ludwig Gieseler observed about the second century Christians:

> Jewish Christians...the *Nazarenes... the millenarianism* of the Jewish Christians...for which the reputation of John (Apoc. xx. 4-6; xxi.) and his peculiar followers, afforded a warrant — this *millenarianism* became the general belief of the time, and met with almost no other opposition than that given by the Gnostics...The thousand years' reign was represented as the great Sabbath which should begin very soon, or as others supposed, after the lapse of the six thousand years of the world's age, with the first resurrection, and should afford great joys to the righteous. Till then the souls of the departed were kept in the underworld, and the opinion that they should be taken up to heaven immediately after death, was considered a gnostic heresy.[187]

It is known that the belief the "Judeo-Christians" held (like those who are part of the Philadelphia remnant of the Church of God) held on the millennium and six-thousand-year plan was adopted by all Christians in the second century and that view was only challenged at that time by false "Christians," called Gnostics.

A Thousand Years is as a Day

Some believe that since God made/recreated the world in six days and rested on the seventh day (Genesis 2:1-3), that humans will have 6,000 years to live on the Earth under Satan's influence, but will have a 1,000 years to be under Christ's reign. The 6,000 plus 1,000 years equals God's seven thousand year plan.

Many have noted that a thousand years seems to be as one day to God. This is a concept from both the Old and New Testaments:

> 4 For a thousand years in Your sight Are like yesterday when it is past (Psalm 90:4).

> 8 But, beloved, do not forget this one thing, that with the Lord one day is as a thousand years, and a thousand years as one day (2 Peter 3:8).

Based upon certain calculations, it seems that Adam and Eve were created and/or apparently left the Garden of Eden between 5,980 to 5,995 years ago (roughly 3974-3989 B.C.). This would mean that when Jesus began to preach, roughly 27 A.D., over four thousand year later, He was preaching in day five, as four of the seven "one thousand year days" would have been over before then.

Thus, days five and six could have been considered as part of the last days by the early disciples.

If that is so, it helps to explain why some New Testament figures indicated that they were in the last days:

> But Peter, standing up with the eleven, raised his voice and said to them, "Men of Judea and all who dwell in Jerusalem, let this be known to you, and heed my words. For these are not drunk, as you suppose, since it is only the third hour of the day. But this is what was spoken by the prophet Joel: '*And it shall come to pass in the last days, says God, That I will pour out of My Spirit on all flesh* (Acts 2:14-17).

> God, who at various times and in various ways spoke in time past to the fathers by the prophets, has **in these last days** spoken to us by His Son, whom He has appointed heir of all things (Hebrews 1:1-2).

If there is no 6,000 year plan of human rule followed by a 1,000 year "millennial" reign, then the New Testament statement above about then being in the *last days* make little semi-literal sense. Since God does have a 7,000 year plan, these statements do make sense. That also explains why the end has not come yet. There is still a little more time in "the last days."

Two Types of Last Days

It also needs to be understood that there are two types

of *last days* referred to in the New Testament.

When some in the New Testament were stating that they were in the last days, this indicates the latter three days of the 7,000 year week.

However in other places, New Testament writers sometimes are referring to the time of the final generation before Jesus returns as being the last days, as they indicate that this is not the same time in which they were writing (cf. 2 Peter 3:3).

James Ussher's Calculations

Many believe that the 6,000 years are up because of some 17th century calculations a historian, James Ussher, made. James Ussher was then the Anglican Archbishop of Armagh (in what is now Northern Ireland).

Ussher primarily based his calculations upon the chronologies and reigns of kings in the Old Testament to conclude that the world was created in the Fall of 4004 B.C.

There are some problems that can arise from using James Ussher's method:

> 1) The first is that Ussher's method did not seem to take into account that sometimes a son began the reign in a kingdom before his father

king died. One example seems to have started with Solomon, per 1 Kings 1:32-43. Hence, the official chronologies often counted both co-reigns. This could have contributed to possible over-counting by Ussher.

2) It is almost certain that the 6,000 years for humans to rule over themselves apart from direct contact with God began after Adam and Eve sinned and left the Garden of Eden (Genesis 3:24). It could have taken them one day or twenty or more years to sin. The Bible is not specifically clear on this point.

3) James Ussher presumed that Solomon built the Jerusalem Temple in 1012 B.C., but it was likely built decades later.

4) Some claim he also made some biblical calculation errors.[188]

Therefore, people who rely on Ussher's 4004 B.C. calculations to claim that the 6,000 years are up are apparently relying on assumptions, as opposed to fact. But Ussher was somewhat close, and the 6,000 years is ending soon.

Jewish Calculation Concerns

The Jews, on the other hand, tend to believe we have over two centuries left to get to the year 6,000. Why is that?

Theere are various explanations of why. The first is that a Rabbi did a calculation once, made an error, but since it was over 1500 years ago, everyone kept following it. This is possibly the correct reason. Another is that because Josephus in his book *Antiquities of the Jews*, tells that during the time of Seth, "They also were the inventors of that peculiar sort of wisdom which is concerned with the heavenly bodies, and their order,"[189] some calculations started based upon a presumed date for that. Now, that too is likely to be a tradition. But essentially the tradition seems to be that once the ancients started to pay attention to what we know call astronomy, they began counting from then. And this tradition was passed down and/or recorded somewhere and it somehow came into general use.

But again, it is a little unclear. The numbers in the Bible are much clearer and I do not believe that they would be off by over 200 years because of overlapping reigns, differences in birth dates, etc. There is a 1997 book written by an attorney and Orthodox Jew titled *Jewish History in Conflict: A Study of the Major Discrepancy between Rabbinic and Conventional Chronology* with detailed explanations that tries to resolve all of this. Basically, the book suggests that there was a misunderstanding about certain Persian kings and Daniel 9:24-27 and that this error was carried forward. The book's author, Michael First, essentially shows that the current Jewish chronology is flawed and that something closer to the conventional chronology (like this chapter uses) is the correct one, and others have come to similar conclusions. [190]

But irrespective of why, the Jewish year seems to be off by a couple of centuries compared to historical records and the biblical account.

Did Second, Third, and Fourth Century Writers Teach the Six-Thousand-Year Plan?

The idea that God essentially had a 7,000 year plan, with 6,000 years for humans to rule themselves nearly cutoff from God's rule, followed by a one-thousand-year reign by Christ on the planet is found in several early post-New Testament writings.

Although Christians do not consider that the so-called *Epistle of Barnabas* was divinely-inspired, it does show that in the early second century some did understand the idea of a 6,000 year plan followed by the thousand year reign of Christ:

> Moreover concerning the Sabbath likewise it is written in the "Ten Words", in which He spoke to Moses face to face on Mount Sinai: "And sanctify the Lord's Sabbath with clean hands and clean heart." And in another place he says: "If my sons guard the Sabbath then I will bestow my mercy upon them." He speaks of the Sabbath in the beginning of the creation: "And God made the works of his hands in six days, and finished on the seventh day, and rested on it, and sanctified it." Observe, children, what "he finished in six days" means. He means this: that in six thousand years the Lord will bring everything to an end, for the day with him signifies a thousand years. And

he himself bears me witness, saying: "Behold, the day of the Lord will be as a thousand years." Therefore, children, in six days — that is, in six thousand years — everything will be brought to an end. "And he rested on the seventh day." This means when his Son comes, he will abolish the time of the lawless one, and will judge the ungodly, and will change the sun and the moon and the stars, and then he will truly rest on the seventh day.[191]

The above quote shows that there was a belief among those who professed Christianity that there would be a literal thousand year reign of Christ on the Earth, and a 6,000 year plan for humans prior to that.

Close to the end of the second century, a heretical leader named Bardesan wrote the following:

Bardesan, therefore, an aged man, and one celebrated for his knowledge of events, wrote, in a certain work which was composed by him, concerning the synchronisms with one another of the luminaries of heaven, speaking as follows :-- Two revolutions of Saturn, 60 years; 5 revolutions of Jupiter, 60 years; 40 revolutions of Mars, 60 years; 60 revolutions of the Sun, 60 years; 72 revolutions of Venus, 60 years; 150 revolutions of Mercury, 60 years; 720 revolutions of the Moon, 60 years.

And this," says he, "is one synchronism of them all; that is, the time of one such synchronism of them. So that from hence it appears that to complete too such synchronisms there will be required six thousands of years. Thus :-- 200 revolutions of Saturn, six thousands of years; 500 revolutions of Jupiter, 6 thousands of years; 4 thousand revolutions of Mars, 6 thousands of years; Six thousand revolutions of the Sun, 6 thousands of years." 7 thousand and 200 revolutions of Venus, 6 thousands of years; 12 thousand revolutions of Mercury, 6 thousands of years." 72 thousand revolutions of the Moon, 6 thousands of years."

These things did Bardesan thus compute when desiring to show that this world would stand only six thousands of years.[192]

He felt that the world would last 6,000 years.

Bishop Irenaeus, another heretical leader, but one that Roman and Orthodox Catholics consider to be a saint, taught about the 6,000 year plan:

For in as many days as this world was made, in so many thousand years shall it be concluded...and in six days created things were completed: it is evident, therefore, that they will come to an end at the sixth thousand year...Thus, then, the six hundred years of Noah, in whose time the deluge occurred because of the apostasy, and the number of the cubits of the image for which these just men were sent into the fiery furnace, do indicate the number of the name of that man in whom is concentrated the whole apostasy of six

132

thousand years, and unrighteousness, and wickedness, and false prophecy, and deception.[193]

Irenaeus is basically trying to say that the creation shows the plan. Irenaeus is also teaching that since God gave Noah 600 years prior to the flood, that humans were given 6,000 years to live in a time of apostasy, essentially cut-off from God (cf. Genesis 3:22-24).

Hippolytus was, and is still considered to have been, an important Roman Catholic leader. He even has his own Catholic feast day.[194] Notice what he wrote:

> And 6,000 years must needs be accomplished, in order that the Sabbath may come, the rest, the holy day "on which God rested from all His works." For the Sabbath is the type and emblem of the future kingdom of the saints, when they "shall reign with Christ," when He comes from heaven, as John says in his Apocalypse: for "a day with the Lord is as a thousand years. "Since, then, in six days God made all things", it follows that 6,000 years must be fulfilled.[195]

Notice, therefore, that one, who is according to Catholic scholars, **"the most important theologian...of the Roman Church in the pre-Constantinian era"**[196] taught the 7,000 year plan (6,000 for humankind, followed by 1,000 from God).

Even though he had other misunderstandings of this doctrine, notice what the Greco-Roman Bishop Victorinus taught in the late 3rd century:

> ...that true and just Sabbath should be observed in the seventh millenary of years. Wherefore to those seven days the Lord attributed to each a thousand years; for thus went the warning: "In Your eyes, O Lord, a thousand years are as one day." Therefore in the eyes of the Lord each thousand of years is ordained, for I find that the Lord's eyes are seven. Wherefore, as I have narrated, that true Sabbath will be in the seventh millenary of years, when Christ with His elect shall reign.[197]

The Greco-Roman Bishop and saint Methodius in the late 3rd or early 4th century taught:

> For since in six days God made the heaven and the earth, and finished the whole world, and rested on the seventh day from all His works which He had made, and blessed the seventh day and sanctified it ... this world shall be terminated at the seventh thousand years, when God shall have completed the world...[198]

In the fourth century, the Greco-Roman supporting Lactantius taught:

> Therefore, since all the works of God were completed in six days, the world must continue in its present state through six ages, that is, six thousand years...And again, since

God, having finished His works, rested the seventh day and blessed it, at the end of the six thousandth year all wickedness must be abolished from the earth, and righteousness reign for a thousand years; and there must be tranquillity and rest from the labours which the world now has long endured…the dead will rise again, not after a thousand years from their death, but that, when again restored to life, they may reign with God a thousand years. For God will come, that, having cleansed the world from all defilement, He may restore the souls of the righteous to their renewed bodies, and raise them to everlasting blessedness.[199]

Commodianus (likely 4th century) wrote:

Adam was the first who fell, and that he might shun the precepts of God, Belial was his tempter by the lust of the palm tree. And he conferred on us also what he did, whether of good or of evil, as being the chief of all that was born from him; and thence we die by his means, as he himself, receding from the divine, became an outcast from theWord. We shall be immortal when six thousand years are accomplished.[200]

Thus, certain second, third, and fourth century leaders, some of whom the Greco-Romans venerate as significant saints, clearly believed in the teaching that there was a 6,000 year plan, (normally believed to be followed by a one thousand year reign).

Many in the Church of God and Some Catholics Understand About the 6.000 Years

Historically, the Church of God seems to have understood that God has given humankind 6,000 years, like the six days of the physical creation, to live cut off from God. This will be followed by the 1,000 year millennial reign, like the seventh day which was created by God's rest, of Christ.

Herbert Armstrong wrote:

> Man built his world on self-sufficiency without God.
>
> God set in motion a master plan for accomplishment of his purpose, consisting of a duration of seven thousand years. Satan was allowed to remain on earth's throne for the first six thousand years. God purposed that man must learn his lesson, and come voluntarily to accept God's way and character.
>
> For nearly six thousand years mankind has been writing that lesson. But even at this late hour he has not yet learned it. He has not yet given up on his own self-centered way and come to accept God's way to his ultimate happiness.[201]

This view is not unique to Herbert Armstrong. G.G. Rupert, a late Church of God leader for another example, taught the 6,000 year plan followed by a 1,000 year millennium.[202]

Furthemore, according to Roman Catholics, at least parts of this view have long been the belief of those who claim to believe at least parts of the Bible even into the 20th century:

> *E. Culligan* (20th century): The saints are then to reign with Christ a thousand years...Many early Christians took this as a literal description...This belief was common in the Early Church...

> ...the time of the First Resurrection will end...It is the time when the Seventh Millennium will set in, and will be the day of Sabbath in the plan of creation...**It has been the common opinion among Jews, Gentiles, and Latin and Greek Christians**, that the present evil world will last no more than 6,000 years...Christians and Jews, from the beginning of Christianity, and before, have taught that 6,000 years after the creation of Adam and Eve, the consummation will occur. The period after the consummation is to be the seventh day of creation--the Sabbath...St. Jerome said, "It is a common belief that the world will last 6,000 years."...

> I believe that as the last days come to an end so will the sixth day of creation.[203]

> *Priest G. Rossi* (19th century): One day with the Lord, then, is as a thousand years, and a thousand years as one day. It is the common interpretation that each of the six days of

creation is equivalent to one thousand years for the future existence of human generations. Now God employed six days in the creation of this world; this world, then, shall last only six thousand years; the Sabbath, or seventh day, representing eternity. The learned Cornelius A. Lapide, in his erudite commentaries on the Bible, in the second chapter of Genesis and twentieth chapter of the Apocalypse, attests that it is a common opinion among Jews and Gentiles, among Latin and Greek Christians, that this world shall last only six thousand years... The same belief is affirmed by St. Gaudentius, the learned and holy Bishop of Brescia and great friend of St. Ambrose, both Fathers of the Church.

"We expect," he says, "that truly holy day of the seventh thousand years, that shall come after those six days, or six thousand years of time, which, being finished, shall begin that holy rest for all true saints and for all those faithful believers in the resurrection of Jesus Christ." (Tract. 10.)[204]

This 6,000 year time period, which some Catholics have held to throughout history (C. Lapide died in the 17th century and Gaudentius the 5th), is almost over. We are in the end times that are leading up to the millennium. Notice that this was considered a "common opinion."

A Catholic monk, sometimes called "the venerable Bede," indicated that the creation was in 3952 B.C.[205]

And thus, even with this date, the 6,000 years would be close to being up. Other Catholics have thought that the 6,000 years would have been over in the late 20th or early 21st century (e.g. Culligan).

However, after Bishop Ratzinger became more influential, he took steps to stop the Catholic Church from endorsing any millennial teachings. Currently the Catholic Church does not teach a 6,000 year plan (even though Pope Paul VI seemed to endorse it and some version of millenarianism in 1966[206]).

The late John Ogwyn wrote a document that indicates that the creation was approximately 3983 B.C. Notice some of the biblically-based math that leads to that conclusion:

> Do Genesis 5:3-29 and 7:11 show that 1,656 years transpired between the creation of Adam and the Flood of Noah's day? Note: Genesis 5:3 shows that Adam was 130 when Seth was born. Add up the age of each patriarch at the birth of his son, plus the age of Noah at the time of the Flood.
>
> Do Genesis 11:10-32 show that 427 years passed between the Flood and the death of Terah, which was the time that Abram left Haran (cf. Acts 7:4)? Was Abram 75 years of age when he left Haran? Genesis 12:4
>
> How old was Abraham when God made the covenant of circumcision with him? Genesis 17:1-10. Had 24 years passed since he left

Haran? Note: A careful comparison of Genesis 12:4 with Genesis 17:1 will reveal Abraham's age at the time of the covenant.

According to Galatians 3:16-17, how many years passed between the time of the covenant with Abraham and the Sinai covenant, which was the year of the Exodus? (cf. Exodus 12:40)...

How many years were there between the Exodus and the fourth year of King Solomon when the temple was begun? 1 Kings 6:1. By using secular records most scholars date the fourth year of Solomon to approximately 966 BC.

If you add the numbers (1,656 + 427 + 24 + 430 + 480 + 966) what would have been the approximate year bc of Adam's creation?

Would this not prove that 6,000 years will soon have elapsed?[207]

Galatians 3:17, which is cited, but without showing the years above, shows four hundred and thirty years. 1 Kings 6:1 shows four hundred and eighty years from the time the children of Israel left Egypt until the fourth year of Solomon's reign. (For more explanation of Terah's age, please see the note related to Abraham.[208])

Therefore, if we add up 1,656 + 427 + 24 + 430 + 480 + 966, this suggests the creation of Adam was around 3983 B.C. Yet years of life are not exact. Since few people are born and die precisely on the same calendar date, and some of the calculation may suggest that, there could possibly be 10 or more additional years past what it suggests (2018). Also, there could be one more year for the "Day of the Lord" (Isaiah 34:8).

As shown, this calculation from John Ogwyn is based upon Adam's total age (as opposed to when he left Eden) and also has not been adjusted for various factors (like co-regencies of kings). As I do not believe that Jesus can come before 2020 (and likely later), John Ogywn's reporting should be considered as his complilation of biblical chronology, provided for the purpose (which he seemed to indicate) to highlight the fact that the end of the 6,000 years was relatively soon. And he was correct about that.

The Date of Solomon's Reign

As the John Ogwyn writing indicated, this calculation is partially dependent upon an estimate of scholars pointing to a 966 B.C. temple dedication, as the work of other scholars indicates that the separation of Israel from Judah was possibly 931 B.C.[209] This separation happened shortly after (1 Kings 11:43; 12:1–20) Solomon's forty-year reign (1 Kings 11:42). Therefore, it would seem that one less year could be indicated (966+4-40=930 B.C. vs. 931 B.C.).

While 966 B.C. is an estimated temple construction date, there are several others who believed Solomon's reign began in 970, hence would come up with a 966 construction date four years later. Here are some references:

> *Jesse Long*: Working back from these dates and the biblical references to the reigns of the kings of Israel and Judah (78 years from the death of Ahab in 853/852 BC) the Kingdom of Solomon was divided in 931/930 BC, at the ascension of Rehoboam to the throne of Israel following the death of Solomon. Since Solomon reigned forty years (v. 42), he must have ascended the throne in 971/970 B.C.[210]

> *Edwin Thiele*: Rehoboam of Judah succeeded Solomon between Tishri 931 and Tishri 930.[211]

> *John Canning*: SOLOMON (Reigned c. 970–c. 932 Bc)[212]

> *Leon Wood & David O'Brien*: SOLOMON THE KING Solomon's reign was long, lasting forty years (970–931) as had his father's before him.[213]

> *Israel Finkelstein & Neil Silberman*: Solomon 40 C. 970–931 BCE.[214]

While there is some controversy related to particulars of any calculation, let's look at the 3983 B.C. date, while understanding not precisely accurate as the actual starting point for the 6,000 years.

What Year is it Now? What Year May be the End?

If one starts from the year 2013 A.D. and adds 3983

years, this adds up to 5996 (5997 for 2014, etc.). However, because there was no year zero (for the transition between B.C. and A.D.), this make 2013 year 5995. Thus, if 2983 was the correct starting point, the 6,000 years would be up about 5 years from 2013 (2013 plus 5 would be the year 2018). Since the seven-year deal of Daniel 9:27 has not yet been confirmed, 2020 is the earliest possible date (presuming no "Day of the Lord" issues) and of course some time later if the deal is not confirmed in 2013.

(While we in the *Continuing* Church of God do believe that God gave humankind 6,000 years to live apart from Him, this does not mean that the universe itself has to be no more than 6,000 years old. The Bible allows for a period of time prior to the creation of humans, cf. Genesis 1:2 and Isaiah 45:18. Therefore, this position is consistent with various scientific observations.)

However, it is important to note that the Bible shows that the days will apparently need to be shortened:

> 22 And unless those days were shortened, no flesh would be saved; but for the elect's sake those days will be shortened (Matthew 24:22).

While 2020 *may* possibly be the end of the 6,000 years, it is possible that it may be one or more years earlier or even ten or so years later as the begettal dates are not exact years and there are co-regency issues for the kings. And the Great Tribulation may or may not begin 3½ years before then. Thus, the Great Tribulation may begin as early as 2017–2020 (or later).

(However, the Great Tribulation cannot be before 2016, as the deal in Daniel 9:27 had not been reported prior to the publishing of this text in 2013.)

Thus, according to a variety of sources, but mainly the Bible, the 6,000 years will be up in the twenty-first century — and probably fairly soon. This will lead to the return of Jesus Christ and the real age of peace. This time also leads to the time of the final pope, who appears to be a type of antipope.

Non-biblical Sources

Interestingly, there are some other Roman Catholic prophecies that state or indicate that the end will occur shortly from now:

> *Ven. Sor Marianne de Jesus Torres* (17th century)...Our Lady told Sister Marianne:...But this knowledge will only become known to the general public in the 20th Century. During this epoch the Church will find herself attacked by waves of the secret sect..."Know, beloved daughter, that when your name is made known in the 20th Century, there will be many who do not believe, claiming this devotion is not pleasing to God...[215]

> *St. John of the Cleft Rock* (14th century): It is said that 20 centuries after the incarnation of the Word, the Beast in its turn will become man. About the year 2000 A.D., Antichrist will reveal himself to the world.[216]

E. Culligan (20th century): The author feels that there is convincing evidence for him to accept that the Antichrist was born on February 5, 1962.[217]

Some Catholic sources are indicating that something should apparently happen in the early portion of the 21st century.

An archbishop seemed to have a similar view that the last days of this current era began in the 20th century:

> *Archbishop Fulton Sheen* (1950): We are living in the days of the Apocalypse--the last days of our era.... The two great forces of the Mystical Body of Christ and the Mystical Body of Antichrist are beginning to draw up the battle lines for the catastrophic contest.[218]

Notice that Archbishop Sheen also was concerned that two great forces were then rising up. Could this be between the faithful Christians and an ecumenically-oriented religion? Fulton Sheen made this statement shortly after the Church of Rome took a stand against the millennial teachings of the Bible) and the Philadelphia era of the Church of God (Revelation 3:7-12) had started to more publicly rise up.

Furthermore, notice two accounts about a pontiff who had a vision in 1884:

> Pope Leo XIII had a vision of a confrontation between God and Satan. Pope Leo was made to

understand that Satan would be allowed one hundred years to tempt and try to destroy the Church. In the vision, Satan chose for his one hundred years the Twentieth Century.[219]

Pope Leo XIII had a remarkable vision...When asked what had happened, he explained that, as he was about to leave the foot of the altar, he suddenly heard voices - two voices, one kind and gentle, the other guttural and harsh. They seemed to come from near the tabernacle. As he listened, he heard the following conversation:

The guttural voice, the voice of Satan in his pride, boasting to Our Lord: "I can destroy your Church."

The gentle voice of Our Lord: "You can? Then go ahead and do so."

Satan: "To do so, I need more time and more power."

Our Lord: "How much time? How much power?"

Satan: "75 to 100 years, and a greater power over those who will give themselves over to my service."

Our Lord: "You have the time, you will have the power. Do with them what you will."[220]

If the 20th century alone was meant in the vision, then the Pope's vision was completely false (as opposed to being a reverse mirror image of God's plan as some private prophecies seem to be). In order for the above to fit in with other Catholic private prophecies, it would probably need to be interpreted that the seventy-five to one hundred years started at about the same time as the time frame as that indicated by Nun Emmerich. If so, the seventy-five years ended in 2008, and the outside date (based on one hundred years) would be about 2033. Unless this Pope had it completely wrong, some part of the end would seem to occur fairly soon.

Greek Eastern Orthodox scholar H. Tzima Otto has claimed that the "Great Monarch," Antichrist, and the antipope are alive now, hence these end time players, according to her, must also be in place in their roles in the 21st century.[221]

Additionally, the European Union has formed, it is also growing, it has its own currency, and is developing its military capabilities. It has set various records since it began to test its Large Hadron Collider (LHC). The LHC project has attracted the world's leading physicists to support Europe's quest to become the world leader in various technologies. The *New York Times* aptly reported that LHC will help produce:

> Those spinoffs now will invigorate the careers and labs of Europe, not the United States, pointed out Steven Weinberg, a physicist at the University of Texas in Austin, who won the

Nobel Prize for work that will be tested in the new collider. Americans will work at CERN, but not as leaders, he said in an e-mail interview.

"There is also a depressing symbolism," he added, "in the fact that the hottest new results in fundamental physics will for decades not be coming from our country."[222]

It is quite possible that this LHC project (or similar ones, such as Germany's FAIR project) will help Europe to develop the military technology to fulfill the prophecy:

4 Who is like the beast? Who is able to make war with him? (Revelation 13:4).

Additionally, the Europeans have been working on their own GPS like system called Galileo. This system will be also used by the Europeans for military purposes and should be at least partially operational by 2014 or so and fully operational later.[223] This type of system will allow Europe to better launch surprise attacks against others, such as the Anglo-American powers; the fact that the USA will partially rely on it,[224] will give the Europeans a unique military capability that the USA will likely regret (Daniel 11:39). Yet apparently the coming King of the South will not think Europe will be too powerful, but that will be an error (Daniel 11:40).

The Bible, early writings, and even Roman Catholic sources confirm that many who professed Christ in the early years taught that God seems to have a 6,000 year plan followed by a literal thousand year millennial reign of Christ.

According to certain Catholic and Church of God sources, the last days of the 6,000 years for humanity to rule itself are almost over. Recent news events indicate that the Europeans should have the military capabilities to fulfill some of the prophecies related to the Beast relatively soon.

With the timing of his papacy, Pope Francis I could be the last pope and antipope, presuming he lives long enough, and ends up performing various miraculous appearing signs.

11. What Can One Expect from the Last Pope?

What can be expected to occur from, or at least partially because of, the last pope?

We can expect deception, signs and lying wonders, forced false worship, persecution, the destruction of the United States of America and its Anglo-descended allies (such as the United Kingdom, Canada, Australia, and New Zealand), a temporary increase in world wealth, the gathering of armies at Armageddon, and the near total destruction of human life on planet earth.

This chapter will quote some specific prophecies on this as well as refer to some previously cited.

Deception

1 John 2:22 states the the antichrist is a liar, while 2 John 7 refers to him as a deceiver (NKJV) or seducer (DRB). Thus, the last pope will be a deceiver.

Jesus taught the source of lies and that those who would not listen to the truth had the devil as their father:

> 42. JESUS therefore said to them, If God were your father: verily you would love me. for from God I proceeded, and came: for I came not of myself, but he sent me: 43. Why do you not know my speech? Because you can not hear my word. 44. You are of your father the

Devil, and the desires of your father you will do. he was a mankiller from the beginning, and he stood not in the verity: because verity is not in him. when he speaketh a lie, he speaketh of his own, because he is a liar, and the father thereof.

45. But because I say the verity, you believe me not. 46. Which of you shall argue me of sin? If I say the verity: why do you not believe me? 47. He that is of God, heareth the words of God. (John 8:42-47, DRB)

Those whose father is the devil believe traditions and their own opinions over the teachings of the word of God. Those who follow the last pope will be believing falsehoods over the true words of God.

He Will be a False Prophet

The Bible refers to a particular individual as the "false prophet" in the Book of Revelation (Revelation 16:13; 19:20; 20:10).

This leader will thus make false prophecies. While the Bible does not specify them, it certainly implies that he will somehow prophesy in such a deceptive way that the nations will gather to fight Jesus ().

This does not mean that the last pope may not make prophecies that do come to pass. Actually, I expect that he will. But the Bible also warns that even if some prophet makes prophecies that come to pass, if he is advocating false worship, which the last pope will do, that God's people should not listen to him (Deuteronomy 13:1-4).

Signs and Lying Wonders

Sacred scripture teaches "7 For we walk by faith, and not by sight" (2 Corinthians 5:7, DRB).

Yet it also warns that those who do not have "the love of the truth" will fall for signs and lying wonders.

Here are Catholic and Protestant translations of some passages about that:

> 7. For now the mystery of iniquity worketh: only that he which now holdeth, do hold, until he be taken out of the way.
>
> 8. And then that wicked one shall be revealed whom our Lord JESUS shall kill with the spirit of his mouth: and shall destroy with the manifestation of his advent, him, 9. Whose coming is according to the operation of Satan, in all power, and lying signs and wonders,
>
> 10. And in all seducing of iniquity to them that perish, for that they have not received the charity of the truth that they might be saved. 11. Therefore God will send them the operation of error, to believe lying: 12. That all may be judged which have not believed the truth, but have consented to iniquity. (2 Thessalonians 2:7-12, DRB)

7 For the mystery of lawlessness is already at work; only He who now restrains will do so until He is taken out of the way.

8 And then the lawless one will be revealed, whom the Lord will consume with the breath of His mouth and destroy with the brightness of His coming. 9 The coming of the lawless one is according to the working of Satan, with all power, signs, and lying wonders, 10 and with all unrighteous deception among those who perish, because they did not receive the love of the truth, that they might be saved.

11 And for this reason God will send them strong delusion, that they should believe the lie, 12 that they all may be condemned who did not believe the truth but had pleasure in unrighteousness.   (2 Thessalonians 2:7-12, NKJV)

So the above verses teach that the mystery of iniquity/lawlessness has been working since Paul's time.   Simon Magus was told by the Apostle Peter that he was bound in iniquity (Acts 8:18).   And most that profess Christ have adopted some of the forms of iniquity he and his followers practiced.

Catholic prophecies show that a pope will have the gift of miracles and perform "prodigies"(see chapter 6).   Since this has not really happened before, this would seem to be a reference to the last pope.

The final Antichrist will perform signs and wonders. This will result in most believing the lie. Misleading is something that the last pope would do.

False Worship

The last pope will promote false worship.

> 12 And he exercises all the authority of the first beast in his presence, and causes the earth and those who dwell in it to worship the first beast, whose deadly wound was healed. 13 He performs great signs, so that he even makes fire come down from heaven on the earth in the sight of men. 14 And he deceives those who dwell on the earth by those signs which he was granted to do in the sight of the beast, telling those who dwell on the earth to make an image to the beast who was wounded by the sword and lived. (Revelation 13:12-14)

At first, it is possible that some type of image with a cross will be used as most who profess Christ will not consider this to be a threat. People will not consider that keeping Sunday enforcement or cross-related images are a turning away of the religion that many believe is Christianity.

But ultimately the final Antichrist/last pope will push people more towards worship of the Beast himself as the above shows.

When some "traditional" religionists object to this (combined with events in the Book of Revelation dealing with the various seals and trumpets related to the Day of the Lord), their objections will likely be a reason that the last pope will go along with the supporters of the Beast that will turn against and destroy Rome (Revelation 17:9-18).

Persecution

The final Antichrist/last pope will be involved in severe persecution:

> 15 He was granted power to give breath to the image of the beast, that the image of the beast should both speak and cause as many as would not worship the image of the beast to be killed. 16 He causes all, both small and great, rich and poor, free and slave, to receive a mark on their right hand or on their foreheads, 17 and that no one may buy or sell except one who has the mark or the name of the beast, or the number of his name.   (Revelation 13:15-17)

So there will be physical and economic persecution of those who will not comply with the Antichrist's demands.

Satan the Dragon (Revelation 12:9) will influence the Beast and the Antichrist to persecute true Christians just prior to the beginning of the Great Tribulation as well as the non-protected Christians after the start of the Great Tribulation:

> 25 He shall speak pompous words against the Most High, Shall persecute the saints of the

Most High, And shall intend to change times and law. Then the saints shall be given into his hand For a time and times and half a time. (Daniel 7:25)

7 "Up, Zion! Escape, you who dwell with the daughter of Babylon." (Zechariah 2:7)

13 Now when the dragon saw that he had been cast to the earth, he persecuted the woman who gave birth to the male Child. 14 But the woman was given two wings of a great eagle, that she might fly into the wilderness to her place, where she is nourished for a time and times and half a time, from the presence of the serpent. 15 So the serpent spewed water out of his mouth like a flood after the woman, that he might cause her to be carried away by the flood. 16 But the earth helped the woman, and the earth opened its mouth and swallowed up the flood which the dragon had spewed out of his mouth. 17 And the dragon was enraged with the woman, and he went to make war with the rest of her offspring, who keep the commandments of God and have the testimony of Jesus Christ. (Revelation 12:13-17)

The Great Tribulation starts with the "time and times and half a time," which is the same length of time a portion of Christians (the continuing "Philadelphian" Christians per Revelation 3:10) are protected/escape (cf. Luke 21:36).

A tribulation of a portion of the faithful, prior to the start of the Great Tribulation, is also prophecied in places such as Daniel 11:28-36, Mark 13:11-13, and Matthew 24:9-10.

Regarding the passages in Daniel 11, the Catholic saint Jerome understood that these passages were referring to the persecution of God's people as his commentary on them included the following:

> But these events were typically prefigured under Antiochus Epiphanes, so that this abominable king who persecuted God's people foreshadows the Antichrist, who is to persecute the people of Christ.[225]

The idea of persecution involving supporters of the Beast and Antichrist has been understood by various theologians and is not a new idea.

The Bible shows that the Antichrist will also encourage the Beast to fulfill the following:

> 23 "And in the latter time of their kingdom, When the transgressors have reached their fullness, A king shall arise, Having fierce features, Who understands sinister schemes. 24 His power shall be mighty, but not by his own power; He shall destroy fearfully, And shall prosper and thrive; He shall destroy the mighty, and also the holy people. (Daniel 8:23-24)

Along with the final Antichrist, the Beast gets his power from Satan (cf. Revelation 16:13). But the final Antichrist also will perform signs and wonders himself for the Beast's benefit (Revelation 13:11-15).

The final Antichrist/last pope will be involved in much persecution.

The Destruction of the United States of America and its Anglo-descended Allies

While the first phase of the persecution will happen prior to the Great Tribulation, there will be other types of persecutions that happen after the Great Tribulation begins. And some have to do with what will happen the Anglo-English peoples. This is the time that is also known as the "time of Jacob's trouble" (Jeremiah 30:7).

There are various passages that show that the Beast power that the Antichrist supports will go against the power of the USA and its Anglo-descended allies. While some consider that impossible, notice the following:

> 39 Thus he shall act against the strongest fortresses with a foreign god, which he shall acknowledge, and advance its glory; and he shall cause them to rule over many, and divide the land for gain. (Daniel 11:39)

Who has the "strongest fortresses" in the 21st century? Is it not the United States of America? Once it and its Anglo-allies are taken over and their lands divided, this will help prosper much of the world. It will also lead to persecution of the people of those lands — whether Christian or not.

When the Bible elsewhere shows that the Beast "shall destroy many in their prosperity (Daniel 8:25), this also would seem to at least include the USA and its Anglo-descended allies.

Interestingly, there seem to be several Catholic private prophecies that also foretell the destruction of the English-speaking peoples. And since the last pope will, at least for a while, claim to be Catholic, he may decide to partially rely on them to help justify eliminating the USA and its Anglo-allies.

It should be noted, however, that many of the older Roman Catholic prophecies that mention the "English" were written before that area was actually called England, but was made up of territories of Anglo-Saxon peoples. Of course, if any apply to the U.S.A., Canada, Australia, and/or New Zealand, they were not formed as we now understand them until several centuries after some of the Roman Catholic prophecies were first written. So, although there are errors/distortions in translations, they do seem to somehow refer to the British-American descended peoples. It would seem that they basically were intended to refer to the Anglo-American nations in the twenty-first century.

The following Catholic "private prophecies" appear to predict the destruction of the English:

159

St. Columbkille (597): English nobility shall sink into horrible life—wars shall be proclaimed against them, by means of which the frantically proud race shall be subdued, and will be harassed from every quarter. **The English shall dwindle into disreputable people and shall forever be deprived of power**".[226] ...the **English shall be defeated...they shall be harassed by every quarter**; like a fawn surrounded by a pack of voracious hounds, shall be the position of the English amidst their enemies. The English afterwards shall dwindle down to a disreputable people.[227]

Mother Shipton (died 1551): The time will come when England shall tremble and quake...**London shall be destroyed forever after** . . . and then York shall be London and the Kingdom governed by three Lords appointed by a Royal Great monarch...who will set England right and drive out heresy.[228]

Saint Edward (died 1066): **The extreme corruption and wickedness of the English nation has provoked the just anger of God**. When malice shall have reached the fullness of its measure, God will, in His wrath, send to the English people wicked spirits, who will punish and afflict them with great severity...[229]

Saint Malachy (12th century): ...the English in turn must suffer severe chastisement. Ireland, however, will be instrumental in bringing back the English to the unity of Faith.[230]

Saint Cataldus of Tarentino (c. 500): **The Great Monarch** will be in war till he is forty years of age.......he will assemble great armies and expel tyrants from his empire. He **will conquer England** and other island empires.[231]

Franciscan Friar of Mount Sinai (died 1840): England will become the scene of the greatest cruelties. **Ireland and Scotland will invade England and destroy it**. The royal family will be driven out and half of the population murdered.[232]

D.A. Birch (20th century Catholic writer): It is interesting to note that the National (Government) of England is foretold to have no role in the return of England to Roman allegiance. As a matter of fact, a number of prophecies specifically state that England will be reevangelized by the French and Irish **after England has suffered a terrible and specific chastisement.**[233]

Priest Paul Kramer (2010): Zachary the Armenian Jew who converted to the Catholic Faith – published in 1854...there would be the war that the prophecy refers to as "the struggle of the strong, against the strong". This empire of the north...will go to war against North America and North America will fall and be conquered and brought into bondage...[234]

> *Werdin d' Otrante* (13th century): "The Great
> Monarch and the Great Pope will precede
> Antichrist...**All the sects will vanish. The
> capital of the world will fall**...The Great
> Monarch will come and restore peace and the
> Pope will share in the victory.[235]

In a sense, the capital of the world is the United
States. Hence it seems to be the U.S.A. that Werdin d'
Otrante was referring to. Notice that Zachary said
there would be a battle against the strong of North
America by the empire of the north. Thus, certain
Catholic prophecies appear to be foretelling the
destruction of the Anglo-American powers,
apparently by their Great Monarch.

Sadly, some may well point to these non-Divinely
inspired writings as partial justification for destroying
the United States and peoples of some of the other
British-descended lands.

It is interesting to note that the Catholic Saint Edward
specifically states that demons will be used to punish
the English peoples (whether the majority of Scots,
etc, will be specifically involved or not can be
debated). This would suggest, that presuming that
the Great Monarch attacks them, the Great Monarch
is on the side of demons — and the Bible is clear that
the King of the North and Antichrist (referred to as
the Beast and False Prophet) are on the side of
demons (Revelation 16:13). This should give all who
call themselves Catholic pause to NOT support
someone who is on the side of demons.

There also was a prophecy from a famous stigmatic (a mystic with blood wounds supposedly reflective of those that Jesus suffered when nailed to the stake):

> *Therese Neumann* (20th century): ... at the end of this century America will be destroyed economically by natural disasters. [236]

Although the date of the last prophecy was false, it should be clear according to a variety of sources claiming Catholicism, the United States and the other English-descended peoples are facing disaster — and apparently relatively soon.

And Bible prophecy suggests that the final Antichrist/last pope will be involved in supporting that destruction.

A Temporary Increase in Worldly Wealth

There will be many reasons that those in the world will not too loudly protest the persecutions and elimination of the Anglo-powers (lack of love, other priorities, fear of the final King of the North, envy, etc.).

One reason could be that much of the world will prosper under the Mystery Babylon system (Revelation 17:5; 18:2-8) involving the end time "daughter of Babylon" (Isaiah 47:1-9; Jeremiah 50:42).

There are various scriptures that coincide with the time of the final Antichrist that show a time of wealth that will end in destruction. Those experiencing the time of wealth will not believe that they will be subject to destruction, but such destruction will happen:

> 24 His power shall be mighty, but not by his own power; He shall destroy fearfully, And shall prosper and thrive...(Daniel 8:24)

> 2 And he cried mightily with a loud voice, saying, "Babylon the great is fallen, is fallen, and has become a dwelling place of demons, a prison for every foul spirit, and a cage for every unclean and hated bird! 3 For all the nations have drunk of the wine of the wrath of her fornication, the kings of the earth have committed fornication with her, and the merchants of the earth have become rich through the abundance of her luxury." (Revelation 18:2-3)

> 26 And as it was in the days of Noah, so it will be also in the days of the Son of Man: 27 They ate, they drank, they married wives, they were given in marriage, until the day that Noah entered the ark, and the flood came and destroyed them all. 28 Likewise as it was also in the days of Lot: They ate, they drank, they bought, they sold, they planted, they built; 29 but on the day that Lot went out of Sodom it rained fire and brimstone from heaven and destroyed them all. 30 Even so will it be in the day when the Son of Man is revealed. (Luke 17:26-30)

Although one would think that people who believe the Bible would not wish to be part of the final Babylon, oddly, there are certain Roman and Orthodox Catholic private prophecies that take the opposite position of sacred scripture.

Andrew the Fool-for-Christ: Now son, how can I relate to you without tears the events of the beginning of sorrows and the end of the world? During the End Times, God will reveal as King a certain poor man...This king will rule...Happiness will reign in the world as it did in the days of Noah. People will become very rich...The entire world will fear this king...he will pursue all persons of the Jewish religion out of Constantinople...and the people will rejoice like in the time of Noah until the deluge came.[237]

Monk Leontios (died 543): Rejoice, oh most unhappy one, oh New Babylon!...You, who are the New Babylon rejoice now on behalf of Zion! New Babylon, dance, bounce and leap greatly, make known even those in Haydes what a Grace you have received. Because that peace which was yours to enjoy in times past, and which God has deprived you of in course of battles, receive it once more from the hand of an Angel...oh, the City of Seven Hills the dominion will be yours.[238]

Abbott Joachim (died 1202)...A remarkable Pope will be seated on the pontifical throne, under special protection of the angels. Holy and full of gentleness, he shall undo all wrong, he shall recover the states of the Church, and reunite the exiled temporal powers. As the only Pastor, he shall reunite the Eastern to the Western Church...This holy Pope shall be both pastor and reformer. Through him the East and West shall be in ever lasting concord. **The city of Babylon shall then be the head and guide of the world. Rome, weakened in temporal power, shall forever preserve her spiritual dominion,** and shall enjoy great peace...At the beginning, in order to bring these happy results, having need of a powerful assistance, this holy Pontiff will ask the cooperation of the generous monarch of France (Great Monarch).[239]

So, the above seems to be promoting an emergence of Babylon, its associated wealth, and suggests that the time of Noah towards the end is good. Those who will rely on that type of positive interpretation as opposed to what the Bible actually teaches will be "loving and believing a lie" (cf. 2 Thessalonians 2:7-11). Notice that Abbot Joachim also teaches that this will happen under the reign of a "remarkable Pope"—this would seem to have to be the last pope. Many will be deceived and/or overlook the deception because of the prosperity.

Notice that certain Catholic scholars clearly understand that this end-time Babylon-Rome is not a good thing:

Priest W. Kurz (21st century): Revelation 18 announces and exults the fall of Babylon-Rome under God's judgment, including the mourning of merchants and sailors over their lost incomes.[240]

Wall Tiles from Ancient Babylon (Joyce Thiel)

Bible-believer should realize that it is not only in the Book of Revelation, but also in Jeremiah that being associated with end time Babylon is to be avoided:

> 6 Flee from the midst of Babylon, And every one save his life! Do not be cut off in her iniquity, For this is the time of the LORD's vengeance; He shall recompense her. 7 Babylon was a golden cup in the LORD's hand, That made all the earth drunk. The nations drank her wine; Therefore the nations are deranged. 8 Babylon has suddenly fallen and been destroyed. (Jeremiah 51:6-8).

Catholic scholars, such as Priest Kurz also hold the view that the Babylon of Jeremiah 51, up to verse 58, is considered to be an end time "Roman Empire."[241] End time Babylon is not something that Christians should wish to be part of—they should avoid it (cf. Revelation 18:4).

Amageddon

Most people familiar with prophecy are familiar with a battle that will be staged in Megiddo, and although it is not actually fought there, it is normally called "the battle of Armageddon" (the hills of Megiddo/Mageddo).

Here is some of what the Bible teaches about it:

> [13] And I saw three unclean spirits like frogs coming out of the mouth of the dragon, out of the mouth of the beast, and out of the mouth of the false prophet. [14] For they are spirits of demons, performing signs, which go out to the kings of the earth and of the whole world, to gather them to the battle of that great day of God Almighty. [15] Behold, I am coming as a thief. Blessed is he who watches, and keeps his garments, lest he walk naked and they see his shame." [16] And they gathered them together to the place called in Hebrew, Armageddon (Revelation 16:13-16).

Notice the the false prophet, the last pope, will be involved in encouraging the armies of the world to gather at Armageddon.

Highway sign indicating the approach to Megiddo Junction, nearby Har Megiddo

These will include peoples of the north and east (Daniel

11:44-45) like Russia (Jeremiah 50:41-43) and like China (Revelation 16:12).

Although the Bible shows that God will win the battle against those who stage their armies in Armageddon (cf. Revelation 19:19-20), a prophetess claimed:

> *Anne   Catherine   Emmerich* (died 1824)...Antichrist will fight a successful battle at Mageddo in Palestine after which seven rulers, from fear, will subject themselves to Antichrist and he will thereafter become lord of the world.[242]

Because the Bible shows that God will win the related battle (see Revelation 19:19–20), and the Bible never says that Antichrist wins any battle of Megiddo, Nun Emmerich apparently misidentified Jesus as Antichrist.

Another prophetess claimed:

Venerable Maria of Agreda (died 1665)...the kings will send armies to the Holy Land, but the Antichrist will slay them all.[243]

Notice that the Bible shows that it is God and NOT Antichrist who wins the battle:

> [17] Then I saw an angel standing in the sun; and he cried with a loud voice, saying to all the birds that fly in the midst of heaven, "Come and gather together for the supper of the great God, [18] that you may eat the flesh of kings, the flesh of captains, the flesh of mighty men, the flesh of horses and of those who sit on them, and the flesh of all people, free and slave, both small and great." [19] **And I saw the beast, the kings of the earth, and their armies, gathered together to make war against Him who sat on the horse and against His army.** [20] **Then the beast was captured, and with him the false prophet** who worked signs in his presence, by which he deceived those who received the mark of the beast and those who worshiped his image. These two were cast alive into the lake of fire burning with brimstone. [21] And the rest were killed with the sword which proceeded from the mouth of Him who sat on the horse. And all the birds were filled with their flesh (Revelation 19:17–21).

Notice that the Beast and the False Prophet both lose that battle — thus, Antichrist is then defeated.

Yet some writers have falsely claimed that after the Great Monarch (the Beast of Revelation) and Great Pontiff are defeated, Antichrist will come:

> *Venerable Bartholomew Holzhauser* (died 1658):...The Sixth Epoch from the Great Monarch until Antichrist. This Sixth Epoch of the Church — 'the time of consolation' — begins with the Holy Pope and the Powerful Emperor, and terminates with the reign of Antichrist.[244]

Yet, the Bible shows that it is Jesus who comes after the Beast and False Prophet, not that "Antichrist" comes after some special monarch and a particular pope.

Jesus will return at the last (the seventh) trumpet blast:

> [16] For the Lord Himself will descend from heaven with a shout, with the voice of an archangel, and with the trumpet of God. And the dead in Christ will rise first. [17] Then we who are alive and remain shall be caught up together with them in the clouds to meet the Lord in the air. And thus we shall always be with the Lord. [18] Therefore comfort one another with these words (1 Thessalonians 4:16-18).

Jesus Christ will then establish His millennial kingdom on the earth. The "secret sect," having been raised up in its entirety (1 Thessalonians 4:16-17), will reign with Christ on the earth (Revelation 5:10) for a thousand years (Revelation 20:6).

Yet, prior to that, the last pope will help deceive people to fight against Him.

Near Total Destruction of Human Life

As previously mentioned, the last pope will be part of the end time "daughter of Babylon" that will be eliminated.

When discussing end time events such as the Great Tribulation, Jesus taught that if God did not intervene, there would be no human saved alive:

> 21 For then there will be great tribulation, such as has not been since the beginning of the world until this time, no, nor ever shall be. 22 And **unless those days were shortened, no flesh would be saved**; but for the elect's sake those days will be shortened.
>
> 23 "Then if anyone says to you, 'Look, here is the Christ!' or 'There!' do not believe it. 24 For false christs and false prophets will rise and show great signs and wonders to deceive, if possible, even the elect. 25 See, I have told you beforehand. (Matthew 24:21-25)

The last pope will be part of the system that will lead to the near complete destruction of human life on this planet.

But God will stop it by again sending His Son:

15 Then the seventh angel sounded: And there were loud voices in heaven, saying, "The kingdoms of this world have become the kingdoms of our Lord and of His Christ, and He shall reign forever and ever!" 16 And the twenty-four elders who sat before God on their thrones fell on their faces and worshiped God, 17 saying:

"We give You thanks, O Lord God Almighty, The One who is and who was and who is to come, Because You have taken Your great power and reigned. 18 The nations were angry, and Your wrath has come, And the time of the dead, that they should be judged, And that You should reward Your servants the prophets and the saints, And those who fear Your name, small and great, And should destroy those who destroy the earth." (Revelation 11:15-18)

Those who will have been involved in destroying the earth will be destroyed themselves. And the Bible specifies that this includes the False Prophet/the last pope as Jesus will have him destroyed after His return (Revelation 19:11-21).

The Bible ends with:

20 He who testifies to these things says, "Surely I am coming quickly."

Amen. Even so, come, Lord Jesus! 21 The grace of our Lord Jesus Christ be with you all. Amen. (Revelation 22:20-21)

12. Concluding Prophetic Summary About the Last Pope

According to Catholic prophecy:

- An antipope will arise.
- A pope will hold an ecumenical council that satisfies heretics and results in a more ecumenical religion being accepted.
- The vast majority of Catholics will accept the antipope.
- A pope that performs miracles will arise.
- People around the world will accept the faith that this miracle-performing pope endorses.
- A pope that supports the "Great Monarch/Prince of the North" will arise.
- The Great Monarch, that the pope supports, will eliminate the Anglo-descended nations.
- The "Great Monarch/Prince of the North," that the pope supports, will eliminate an Islamic confederation.
- A pope will reign with the Great Monarch for around four years.
- The destruction of Rome comes after tribulations that a pope oversees.
- Armies from lands, including Russia and Asia, will gather in Armageddon
- A great judge comes after Rome is destroyed.

According to certain understandings of the Malachy prophecy, Pope Francis I is the last pope and if other Catholic prophecies are correct, those events will happen under his pontificate.

Thus, if all of those are true, Pope Francis I will be an antipope, he will compromise the religion of the Church of Rome, the vast majority of Catholics will accept this modified faith, the tribulation will begin while he is pontiff, Rome will be destroyed towards the end of his pontificate, and a great judge will come.

On the other hand, if the Malachy list is not complete, then we will need to wait for another pontiff/religious leader to fulfill some or all of the above.

Do these Catholic private prophecies have any relationship to biblical prophecy?

According to Bible prophecy:

- A false religious leader will arise.
- This false leader will encourage an ecumenical faith.
- The vast majority of humankind will accept this improper faith.
- A false religious leader will perform signs and lying wonders.
- Nearly all humankind will be deceived by signs and lying wonders.
- The final Antichrist will promote the final "Beast/King of the North" that the Bible warns against.
- The "Beast/King of the North," that the Antichrist supports will destroy the Anglo-descended nations.

- The "Beast/King of the North," will destroy an Arabic confederation.
- The Great Tribulation and Day of the Lord last 3 ½ years.
- A few years after the start of the Great Tribulation, Rome will be destroyed.
- Jesus will come after Rome is destroyed.

While the Bible does not clearly teach that Pope Francis I is that religious leader, the timing of the election of Pope Francis I is consistent with the time period for the end of the age and the rise of the final Antichrist. Although the final reign of Antichrist with the Beast will not start for at least a few years, the Antichrist leader could be in place now.

We are living in the last days, and the last pope will take steps that will lead to the destruction of the world as we know it.

But the good news is that Jesus will return and establish the Kingdom of God — and ultimately there will be a time with no more pain, sorrow, or suffering (Revelation 21:1-4). Until then, the Bible teaches that we can expect to face many tribulations (cf. Acts 14:22), some of which will be brought about by the last pope, who may or may not be Francis I.

END-NOTE References

1 Bander P..The Prophecies of St. Malachy. TAN Books, Rockford (IL), 1973, p. 96

2 Sieczkowski C. St. Malachy Last Pope Prophecy: What Theologians Think About 12th-Century Prediction. Huffington Post, February 14, 2013. http://www.huffingtonpost.com/2013/02/14/st-malachy-last-pope-prophecy-theologians-prediction-_n_2679662.html, viewed 02/27/13

3 Catechism of the Catholic Church, # 67, 102 & 104. Imprimatur Potest +Joseph Cardinal Ratzinger. Doubleday, NY 1995, pp. 28, 35-36

4 ApostoliA. Fatima for Today. Ignatius Press, 2010, p. 165

5 Devine, Arthur. Transcribed by Marie Jutras. Prophecy. The Catholic Encyclopedia, Volume XII. Published 1911. New York: Robert Appleton Company. Nihil Obstat, June 1, 1911. Remy Lafort, S.T.D., Censor. Imprimatur. +John Cardinal Farley, Archbishop of New York

6 Joyce G. H. Transcribed by Gerard Haffner. The Pope. The Catholic Encyclopedia, Volume XII. Copyright © 1911 by Robert Appleton Company. Online Edition Copyright © 2003 by Kevin Knight. Nihil Obstat, June 1, 1911. Remy Lafort, S.T.D., Censor. Imprimatur. +John Cardinal Farley, Archbishop of New York

7 White C. The Emergence of Christianity. Greenwood Publishing Group, 2007 p. 89

8 Kramer HB L. The Book of Destiny. Nihil Obstat: J.S. Considine, O.P., Censor Deputatus. Imprimatur: +Joseph M. Mueller, Bishop of Sioux City, Iowa, January 26, 1956. Reprint TAN Books, Rockford (IL), pp. 318-319; Joyce, George. "The Pope." The Catholic Encyclopedia. Vol. 12. New York: Robert Appleton Company, 1911. 11 Mar. 2013 <http://www.newadvent.org/cathen/12260a.htm>

9 Kramer HB L, pp. 318-319

10 Thiel B. 2012 and the Rise of the Secret Sect. Nazarene Books, 2009, p. 198

[11] Allen J. Profile: Jesuit Bergoglio, was runner-up in 2005 conclave. NCR, March 3, 2013

[12] Allen J. Profile: Jesuit Bergoglio, was runner-up in 2005 conclave. NCR, March 3, 2013

[13] Pope Francis I. Wikpedia, viewed 03/13/13

[14] Allen J. Profile: Jesuit Bergoglio, was runner-up in 2005 conclave. NCR, March 3, 2013

[15] Riva A. Pope Francis I: First Jesuit Pope Shatters Centuries Of Mistrust. International Business Times, March 13, 2013

[16] Martin R. The Most Powerful Man in the World? The "Black" Pope Count Hans Kolvenbach -- The Jesuit's General. The SPECTRUM Newspaper, May 2000, per

http://www.biblebelievers.org.au/blackpope.htmviewed March 13, 2013

[17] Riva A. Pope Francis I: First Jesuit Pope Shatters Centuries Of Mistrust. International Business Times, March 13, 2013

18 Warren V. Catholic Church still plagued by cardinal sin. Washington Post, March 5, 2013. http://www.washingtonpost.com/blogs/guest-voices/post/catholic-church-still-plagued-by-cardinal-sin/2013/03/05/ba6744e4-8532-11e2-98a3-b3db6b9ac586_blog.html

19 Norman J. Groups name "dirty" cardinals ahead of papal conclave. CBS, March 6, 2013. http://www.cbsnews.com/8301-202_162-57572798/groups-name-dirty-cardinals-ahead-of-papal-conclave/

20 Ligourian, Volume 60, 1972, p. 70

21 Owen R. Chief exorcist Father Gabriele Amorth says Devil is in the Vatican. Time Online, March 10, 2010. http://www.timesonline.co.uk/tol/comment/faith/article7056689.ece viewed 03/10/13

22 Ferrara CA. Epilogue, The Still Hidden Secret. Good Counsel Publications, 2010, p. 64; Who Do YOU Believe? Sister Lucy or Cardinal Bertone? The Fatima Crusader, 95, Summer 2010, p. 19

[23] Toth IG. Between Islam and Catholicism: Bosnian Franciscan Missionaries in Turkish Hungary, 1584-1716. The Catholic Historical Review, Volume 89, Number 3, July 2003, pp. 409-433

[24] Connor, Edward. Prophecy for Today. Imprimatur + A.J. Willinger, Bishop of Monterey-Fresno; Reprint: Tan Books and Publishers, Rockford (IL), 1984, p. 36

[25] Glasse C. New Encyclopedia of Islam: A Revised Edition of the Concise Encyclopedia of Islam, 3rd edition, 2008, pp. 143, 316; Ibn Zubair Ali, Mohammed Ali. The minor signs of Last Days from: The Signs of Qiyamah. http://www.islamawareness.net/Prophecies/minor.html viewed 06/21/09

[26] Ibid

27 Newman JH. The Protestant Idea of Antichrist. [British Critic, Oct. 1840]. Newman Reader — Works of John Henry Newman. Copyright © 2004 by The National Institute for Newman Studies. http://www.newmanreader.org/works/essays/volume2/antichrist1.html viewed 12/03/07, p. 117

28 "A Treatise concerning Antichrist, Purgatory, the Invocation of Saints, and the Sacraments" as shown in Jones, William. The history of the Christian church from the birth of Christ to the xviii. century, Volumes 1-2, 3rd edition. R.W. Pomeroy, 1832. Original from Harvard University, Digitized, Feb 6, 2009, pp. 337-340

29 Kurz, p. 68

30 "Antipope." The Catholic Encyclopedia. Vol. 1. New York: Robert Appleton Company, 1907. Nihil Obstat. March 1, 1907. Remy Lafort, S.T.D., Censor. Imprimatur. +John Cardinal Farley, Archbishop of New York. 25 Feb. 2013 <http://www.newadvent.org/cathen/01582a.htm>

31 Ibid.

32 Dupont, pp. 60, 116

33 Dupont, p. 116

34 Emmerich AC. The Life and Revelations of Anne Catherine Emmerich, p.274

35 Ibid, p.130

36 Ibid, p. 344

37 Ibid, p. 346

38 Ibid, p. 353

39 Culligan E. The Last World War and the End of Time. The book was blessed by Pope Paul VI, 1966. TAN Books, Rockford (IL), pp. 173. Note this was approved for publication by the Catholic Bishop of Lecce, Italy in 1879 per Culligan, p. 169

40 Culligan , p. 128

41 Culleton, R. Gerald. The Reign of Antichrist, p. 122

42 Dupont, pp. 34,60-61

43 Culleton, p. 42

44 Connor, p. 87

45 Connor, p. 76

46 Culleton, p. 132

47 Culleton, p. 130

48 Birch, p. 343

49 Berry ES. The Apocalypse of St. John, 1920. Quoted in Culleton RG. The Reign of Antichrist. Reprint 1974, TAN Books, Rockford (IL), p. 195

50 Huchedé, P. Translated by JBD. History of Antichrist. Imprimatur Edward Charles Fabre, Bishop of Montreal. English edition 1884, Reprint 1976. TAN Books, Rockford (IL), p. 24

51 Kramer HBL, p. 319

52 Flynn, p. 255

53 Kramer P. The Pope Proclaims May 13 Feast of Our Lady of Fatima, p. 5

54 Kramer P. The Imminent Chastisement for Not Fulfilling Our Lady's Request. An edited transcript of a speech given at the Ambassadors of Jesus and Mary Seminar in Glendale, California, September 24, 2004. THE FATIMA CRUSADER Issue 80, Summer 2005, pp. 32-45

http://www.fatimacrusader.com/cr80/cr80pg32.asp viewed 4/15/08

55 Kramer P. The Third Secret Reveals the Great Chastisement. The Fatima Crusader, 77, Summer 2004, p. 4

56 Kramer H, pp. 278, 285

57 Birch, p. 343

58 Dupont, p.45

59 Bessieres A. Wife, Mother and Mystic (Blessed Anna Maria Taigi). Nihil Obstat: Carlos Davis, S.T.L. Imprimatur: E Morrough Bernard, Westmonasteri, die Februari, 1952. Reprint TAN Books, Rockford (IL), 1982, p. 166

60 Culleton, The Prophets and Our Times, p. 153

61 Culleton , p. 154

62 Connor, pp. 34-35

63 Birch, p. 555

64 Culleton, pp. 160-162

65 Birch, pp.267-269

66 Birch, p. 276

67 Culleton, The Prophets and Our Times, p. 110

68 Connor, p.37

69 Dupont, p. 115

70 Birch, p. 555

71 Dupont, p. 40

72 Kramer H., pp. 239,241-242

73 Dupont, p.45

74 Birch, 449

75 Connor, p. 38

76 Culleton, The Prophets and Our Times, p. 193

77 Connor, p.25

78 Leo XIII. AD EXTREMAS ON SEMINARIES FOR NATIVE CLERGY. Encyclical of Pope Leo XIII promulgated on June 24, 1893. http://www.vatican.va/holy_father/leo_xiii/encyclicals/documents/hf_l-xiii_enc_24061893_ad-extremas_en.html viewed 07/19/09

79 Kumar, Vijay. End of the World 2012. http://www.godrealized.com/2012.html viewed 01/18/09

80 Hindu Prophecies: The Kalki Purana. http://ww-iii.tripod.com/hindu.htm viewed 04/19/09

81 Pui-Hua, p. 85

82 Pui-Hua, p. 89

83 DR. MENDELEYEFF'S STRIKING PROPHECY, August 11, 1907

84 Devine, Arthur. "Prophecy." The Catholic Encyclopedia. Vol. 12. Nihil Obstat. June 1, 1911. Remy Lafort, S.T.D., Censor. Imprimatur. +John Cardinal Farley, Archbishop of New York. New York: Robert Appleton Company, 1911. 10 Mar. 2009 <http://www.newadvent.org/cathen/12473a.htm>).

85 Dupont, Yves. Catholic Prophecy: The Coming Chastisement. TAN Books, Rockford (IL), 1973, p.19

86 Bander, p. 11

87 Culligan, p. 118

88 Lindsey H. "Benedict Steps Down." The Hal Lindsey Report. TBN, February 17, 2013

89 Zimmer B. Where Did Biden Get His "Bunch of Malarkey"? Visual Thesaurus, August 12, 2012. http://www.visualthesaurus.com/cm/wordroutes/where-did-biden-get-his-bunch-of-malarkey/ viewed 02/27/13

90 Devine, "Prophecy."

91 Sieczkowski C. St. Malachy Last Pope Prophecy: What Theologians Think About 12th-Century Prediction. Huffington Post, February 14, 2013. http://www.huffingtonpost.com/2013/02/14/st-malachy-last-pope-prophecy-theologians-prediction-_n_2679662.html, viewed 02/27/13

92 Donavon CB, STL. Catholic Q&A Our Lady of Garabandal and the next pope: Question from Marie on 04-17-2005. EWTN. http://www.ewtn.com/vexperts/showmessage_print.asp?number=435995&language=en viewed 02/25/13

93 Ibid

94 Bander, pp. 50-54

95 Connor, pp. 7-9

96 Bander, inside cover

97 Bander. p.3

98 Bander. p.94

99 Bander. p.94

100 Bander. p.94

101 Bander. p.94

102 Bander. p.95

103 Bander. p.95

104 Campbell LJ, Priest. De Labore Solis. The Daily Catholic, April 17, 2005, vol. 16, no. 107. http://dailycatholic.org/issue/05Apr/04517qui.htm viewed 03/04/13

105 Bander. p.96

106 Bander. p.96

107 Dupont p. 68

108 Connor, p. 32

109 Dupont, p. 78

110 Nostradamus M. The Complete Prophecies of Nostradamus, Century II, Quatrain 41. Wilder Publications, 2007, p. 28

111 Dupont, pp. 72-73

112 Pianigiani G, Povoledo E. Benedict XVI to Keep His Name and Become Pope Emeritus. New York Times, February 26, 2013. http://www.nytimes.com/2013/02/27/world/europe/benedict-xvi-to-keep-his-name-and-become-pope-emeritus.html?_r=0

113 McGough M. For conservative Catholics, one pope too many. Los Angeles Times, February 26, 2013. http://www.latimes.com/news/opinion/opinion-la/la-ol-pope-benedict-resignation-20130226,0,6964036.story

114 Bander, p.96

115 Devine, Arthur. "Prophecy." The Catholic Encyclopedia. Vol. 12. New York: Robert Appleton Company, 1911. 17 Nov. 2011 <http://www.newadvent.org/cathen/12473a.htm>

116 Rossi, Gaudentius. The Christian Trumpet: Or, Previsions and Predictions about Impending General Calamities, the Universal Triumph of the Church, the Coming of the Anti-Christ, the Last Judgment, and the End of the World; Divided Into Three Parts, 4th edition. Patrick Donahoe, 1875. Original from Oxford University. Digitized Sep 1, 2006, p. 203

117 Duffy, p. 393; Bander p. 54

118 Smith-Spark L, Latza Nadeau B. Big crowds gather for Benedict's final papal audience. CNN, February 27, 2013. http://edition.cnn.com/2013/02/27/world/europe/vatican-pope/?hpt=hp_c1

119 Gurugé A. The Next Pope. Anura Guruge, 2010, p. 221

120 Devine, "Prophecy"

121 Culleton, R. Gerald. The Prophets and Our Times. Nihil Obstat: L. Arvin. Imprimatur: Philip G. Scher, Bishop of Monterey-Fresno, November 15, 1941. Reprint 1974, TAN Books, Rockford (IL), p. 138

122 Gurugé, pp. 221-223

123 Thiel B. Is This Satan's Throne? Church of God News, August 18, 2012. http://www.cogwriter.com/news/wcg-news/is-this-satans-throne/

124 Devine, "Prophecy"

125 Kramer H.B. L. The Book of Destiny, pp. 318,319

126 Maas, Anthony. "Antichrist." The Catholic Encyclopedia. Vol. 1. New York: Robert Appleton Company, 1907. Nihil Obstat. March 1, 1907. Remy Lafort, S.T.D., Censor. Imprimatur. +John Cardinal Farley, Archbishop of New York. 10 Dec. 2008 <http://www.newadvent.org/cathen/01559a.htm>.)

127 Tzima Otto, p. 138

128 Hildegard of Bingen. Scivias. Paulist Press, Mahwah (NJ), pp. 497,498

129 Newman, Barbara. Voice of the Living Light: Hildegard of Bingen and Her World. Published by University of California Press, 1998, p. 83

130 Annotations on The Second Epistle of Saint Paul to the Thessalonians. The Original and True RHEIMS NEW TESTAMENT of Anno Domini 1582 , p. 423

131 Annotations on Chapter 17 of the Apocalypse. The Original And True Rheims New Testament Of Anno Domini 1582, p. 583

132 Tzima Otto, pp. 30, 31, 32, 50-51,52

133 Tzima Otto, p. 60

134 Flynn, p.349

135 Dupont, p.45

136 Connor, p. 37

137 Birch, p. 255

138 Culleton, p. 137

139 Birch, p. 265

140 Tzima Otto, p. 147; Connor, p. 34

141 Van Den Biesen C. Transcribed by Michael C. Tinkler. Apocalypse. The Catholic Encyclopedia, Volume I. Published 1907. New York: Robert Appleton Company. Nihil Obstat, March 1, 1907. Remy Lafort, S.T.D., Censor. Imprimatur. +John Cardinal Farley, Archbishop of New York

142 Connor, p. 73

143 Connor, pp. 31-33

144 Justin. First Apology, Chapter XXVI. Excerpted from Ante-Nicene Fathers, Volume 1. Edited by Alexander Roberts & James Donaldson. American Edition, 1885

145 Tertullian. Translated by Peter Holmes. A Treatise on the Soul, Chapters 34-35. Excerpted from Ante-Nicene Fathers, Volume 3. Edited by Alexander Roberts and James Donaldson. American Edition, 1885.

146 Irenaeus. Adversus haereses, Book 1, Chapter 23

147 Hippolytus. Refutation of All Heresies. Translated by J. H. Machmahon. Excerpted from Ante-Nicene Fathers, Volume 5. Edited by Alexander Roberts & James Donaldson. American Edition, 1886.

148 B. Thiel, Were the Pharisees Condemned for Keeping the Law of God? 1999-2013

http://www.cogwriter.com/pharisee.htm

149 Culleton, The Reign of Antichrist, pp. 141-142

150 Culleton, The Prophets and Our Times, pp. 177-178

151 Culleton, pp. 171,172

152 Birch, pp. 225,226

153 Connor, p. 36

154 Penn L. False dawn: the United Religions Initiative, globalism, and the quest for a one-world religion. Sophia Perennis, 2005, p. 420

155 Homze A, Homze E. Germany: the divided nation. Nelson, 1970, p. 30

156 Ramm B. Holy Roman Empire. World Book Encyclopedia, Vol. 9. Field Enterprises, Chicago, pp. 265-266

157 Luttwak E. The Grand Strategy of the Byzantine Empire, Harvard University Press, 2009, p. 140

158 Otto von Habsburg. The Economist, 400 (8742), July 16, 2011, p. 89

159 Tzima Otto, p. 316

160 Dupont, p. 76

161 McJimsey G. Documentary History of the Franklin D. Roosevelt Administration: FDR's response to German aggression : Czechoslovakia, 1938, Volume 24 of Documentary History of the Franklin D. Roosevelt Administration, University Publications of America, 2005, p. 544

162 Semin M. The European Union: USSR Repackaged. Fatima Crusader, 95, Summer 2010, p. 75

163 The False Prophet. Living in the Final Generation.

http://www.geocities.com/rebornempowered/ApparitionsofMary.htm 10/12/07

164 Kramer H., p. 318,320-323

165 Gerasimos, Bishop. At the End of Time: The Eschatological Expectations of the Church. Holy Cross Orthodox Press. October 5, 2004, pp. 28-29

166 Culleton, p. 50

167 Dupont, p. 33

168 Culleton, The Reign of Antichrist, p. 153

169 Cited in Socci, p. 147

170 Cited in Socci, p. 148

171 Dupont, p.62

172 Dupont, p.62

173 Connor, p. 49

174 Slattery M, Priest. Homily Notes for August. The Furrow, Vol. 28, No. 6 (Jun., 1977), pp. 375-380

175 Priest Parent, quoted by Le Hidec. As cited in THE SECRETS OF LA SALETTE. http://www.crc-internet.org/salette3.htm viewed 09/28/08 (Note: I have also seen this in French in a book titled Les mystères du sang royal: de Charlemagne à Louis XVII, existe-t-il une survivance by Daniel Leveillard)

176 Thiel B. Fatima Shock! Nazarene Books, 2012

177 Pallavicino, lib. 1, cap. 25, pp. 95, 96: "Il gran seguito di Martino; 1' alienazione del popolo d'Alemagna dalla Corte di Roma… e il rischio di perdere la Germania per avarizia d' una moneta." As cited in Wylie J.A. The History of Protestantism. Edinburgh, 1878.

178 Wylie J.A. The Papacy is the Antichrist, A Demonstration. Chapter 1. Edinburgh, 1888. Reprinted, 2003, by Giving & Sharing, Neck City (MO)

179 Walvoord, pp. 515,608,610

180 Bynum EL. Why We Cannot Support The Billy Graham Crusade. Tract # G-603. TABERNACLE BAPTIST CHURCH, Lubbock, Texas

181 Reston M. Pastor John Hagee says he's sorry for anti-Catholic remarks. Los Angeles Times, May 14, 2008

182 Newman JH. The Protestant Idea of Antichrist. [British Critic, Oct. 1840]. Newman Reader — Works of John Henry Newman. Copyright © 2004 by The National Institute for Newman Studies. http://www.newmanreader.org/works/essays/volume2/antichrist1.html viewed 12/03/07, p. 117

183 Spencer M. The coming evangelical collapse. The Christian Science Monitor, from the March 10, 2009 edition. http://www.csmonitor.com/2009/0310/p09s01-coop.html viewed 03/13/09

184 Gibbon E. Decline and Fall of the Roman Empire, Volume I. ca. 1776-1788. The Modern Library, NY, p. 403

185 Babylonian Talmud: Tractate Sanhedrin Folio 97a

186 The Jewish Messiah: Redemption of Israel. Copyright © 2009 Hanefesh: National Assembly of Jewish Students. http://www.hanefesh.com/edu/Messiah.htm viewed 12/22/09

187 Gieseler, Johann Karl Ludwig. A Text-book of Church History. Translated by Samuel Davidson, John Winstanley Hull, Mary A. Robinson. Harper & brothers, 1857, Original from the University of Michigan, Digitized Feb 17, 2006, pp. 128, 166-167

188 Sungenis R. Good News and Bad News Regarding Scriptural Chronologies. Catholic Apologetics International. http://www.catholicintl.com/catholicissues/scriptural-chronologies2.htm viewed 05/12/09

189 Josephus, Book 1, Chapter 2

190 Reagan D. The Jewish Calendar: What year is it, and does it really matter? http://www.lamblion.com/articles/articles_jewishlife3.php viewed 04/02/12

191 Epistle of Barnabas, 15:1-5. In Holmes, p. 315

192 Bardesan. By a certain Philip, disciple of Bardesan. Appendix after The Book of the Laws of Various Countries. Excerpted from Ante-Nicene Fathers, Volume 8. Edited by Alexander Roberts & James Donaldson. American Edition, 1886. Online Edition Copyright © 2004 by K. Knight

193 Irenaeus. Adversus haereses, Book V, Chapter 28, Verse 2 & Chapter 29, Verse 2

194 Kirsch. St. Hippolytus of Rome

195 Hippolytus. On the HexaËmeron, Or Six Days' Work. From Fragments from Commentaries on Various Books of Scripture. http://www.newadvent.org/fathers/0502.htm viewed 9/17/07

196 Kirsch. St. Hippolytus of Rome

197 Victorinus. Commentary on the Creation. Translated by Robert Ernest Wallis. From Ante-Nicene Fathers, Vol. 7. Edited by Alexander Roberts, James Donaldson, and A. Cleveland Coxe. (Buffalo, NY: Christian Literature Publishing Co., 1886.) Revised and edited for New Advent by Kevin Knight

198 Methodius. Banquet of the Ten Virgins (Discourse 9), Chapter 1

199 Lactantius. Divine Institutes, Book VII (Of a Happy Life), Chapters 14, 22. Translated by William Fletcher. From Ante-Nicene Fathers, Vol. 7. Edited by Alexander Roberts, James Donaldson, and A. Cleveland Coxe. (Buffalo, NY: Christian Literature Publishing Co., 1886.) Revised and edited for New Advent by Kevin Knight. <http://www.newadvent.org/fathers/07017.htm>

200 Commodianus. On Christian Discipline, Chapter XXXV. Translated by Robert Ernest Wallis. From Ante-Nicene Fathers, Vol. 4. Edited by Alexander Roberts, James Donaldson, and A. Cleveland Coxe. (Buffalo, NY: Christian Literature Publishing Co., 1885.) Revised and edited for New Advent by Kevin Knight. http://www.newadvent.org/fathers/0411.htm

201 Armstrong HW. Mystery of the Ages. Dodd & Mead, 1985

202 Rupert GG. Time, Tradition, and Truth Concerning the End of the World, 3rd edition. Union Publishing Company, 1918, pp. 26-30

203 Culligan, pp. 113-115; Papal blessing is prior to inside title page

204 Rossi , p. 233

205 Ussher Chronology. Wikipedia. Viewed 9/17/07

206 Culligan, pp. 113-115

207 Bible Study Course. Lesson 2, Part 2, God 7,000-Year Plan. Copyright © 2008. http://online.twbiblecourse.org/bsc_lesson_content.php?lesson=2&page=5 viewed 04/19/08

208 There have been concerns about whether Terah was 70 or 130 when Abram was born. Here is one explanation from J. Sarfati, "Note that Abraham was not Terah's firstborn. Gen. 12:4 says Abraham was 75 when he left Haran, and this was soon after Terah died at 205 (Gen. 11:32), and the difference (205–75) means Terah was actually 130 years old when Abraham was born, not 70 (Ussher seems to have been the first modern chronologist to have noticed this point). The latter figure refers to Terah's age when the oldest of the three sons mentioned was born, probably Haran." Sarfati J. Journal of Creation 17(3):14–18 December 2003. http://creation.com/biblical-chronogenealogies viewed 05/23/09)

209 Thiele E. The Mysterious Numbers of the Hebrew Kings. Kregel Publications version, 1994, p. 80

210 Long, Jesse. 1 & 2 Kings: 1 and 2 Kings. College Press, 2002, p. 156

211 Thiele, p. 80

212 Canning, John. 100 Great Kings, Queens, and Rulers of the World. Taplinger Pub. Co., 1967, p. 52

213 Wood L, O'Brien D. A Survey of Israel's History. Zondervan, 1986, p. 253

214 Israel I, Silberman. N. David and Solomon: In Search of the Bible's Sacred Kings and the Roots of the Western Tradition. Simon and Schuster, 2007, p. 20

215 Birch, pp. 317,326

216 Dupont, p. 23

217 Culligan pp. 100-101

218 Flynn T & M. The Thunder of Justice. Maxkol Communications, Sterling (VA), 1993, p. 20

219 Flynn, pp. 4-5

220 The Vision Of Pope Leo XIII, October 13, 1884 http://www.stjosephschurch.net/leoxiii.htm viewed 02/25/09

221 Tzima Otto, H. The Great Monarch and WWIII in Orthodox, Roman Catholic and Scriptural Prophecies. Verenikia Press, Rock Hill (SC), 2000, pp. xxii, 471

222 Overbye D. Collider Sets Record, and Europe Takes U.S.'s Lead. New York Time, December 9, 2009. http://www.nytimes.com/2009/12/10/science/10collide.html viewed 12/11/09

223 EU says satellite navigation system expected to be partly operational by the end of 2014. Washington Post, September 6, 2012

224 U.S. and the EU to collaborate on usage of Global Navigation Satellite Systems. BNO News, July 31, 2010. http://wireupdate.com/local/u-s-and-the-eu-to-collaborate-on-usage-of-global-navigation-satellite-systems/

225 Jerome. Commentary on Daniel, Chapter 11. Translated by Gleason L. Archer. (1958). This text was transcribed by Roger Pearse, Ipswich, UK, 2004. http://www.ccel.org/ccel/pearse/morefathers/files/jerome_daniel_02_text.htm viewed 06/05/11

226 Culligan, pp. 118-119

227 Culleton, The Prophets and Our Times, pp. 131,132

228 Culleton, The Prophets and Our Times, p. 163

229 Culleton, The Prophets and Our Times, p. 137

230 Dupont, p.15

231 Connor, p.30

232 Culleton, The Reign of Antichrist. Reprint TAN Books, Rockford, IL, 1974., p. 163

233 Birch, pp. 308-309

234 Kramer P. What are the missing contents of the third secret? Fatima Crusader, 95. Summer 20120, pp, 45-46

235 Connor, p. 33

236 Flynn, p. A259

237 Tzima Otto, pp. 111, 113,114

238 Tzima Otto, pp. 82-83

239 Connor, pp. 31-32

240 Kurz, p. 166

241 Kurz, pp. 48-49

242 Connor, p. 86

243 Connor, p. 84

244 Connor, pp.35-36

Free Newsletter

Those who wish to get a free, and essentially daily, email newsletter of news events from Dr. Thiel can sign up for that at:

http://www.cogwriter.com/news/

YouTube

Dr. Thiel is on YouTube channel **BibleNewsProphecy**
http://www.youtube.com/BibleNewsProphecy

Made in the USA
Lexington, KY
29 September 2015